BARKING, BEGGING, DIGGING, CHEWING, CHASING, JUMPING . . .

Dogs are a delight—but when their behavior gets out of hand, they can be difficult to deal with. Animal expert Mordecai Siegal offers training tips and tricks to help you solve your dog's problems—with understanding and love.

SOLUTIONS FOR . . .

- HOUSEBREAKING "ACCIDENTS"
- AGGRESSIVENESS
- FEARFULNESS
- DESTRUCTIVE BEHAVIOR
- SEPARATION ANXIETY

AND MORE

UNDERSTANDING THE DOG YOU LOVE

Also from Berkley Books

UNDERSTANDING THE DOG YOU LOVE

MORDECAI SIEGAL

BERKLEY BOOKS, NEW YORK

For Don Gantry,
who thought lovingly of his dog to the end,
and whom I miss very much.

UNDERSTANDING THE DOG YOU LOVE

A Berkley Book / published by arrangement with
the author

PRINTING HISTORY
Berkley edition / May 1994

All rights reserved.
Copyright © 1994 by Mordecai Siegal.
This book may not be reproduced in whole
or in part, by mimeograph or any other means,
without permission. For information address:
The Berkley Publishing Group,
200 Madison Avenue,
New York, New York 10016.

ISBN: 0-425-14234-5

BERKLEY®
Berkley Books are published by
The Berkley Publishing Group, 200 Madison Avenue,
New York, New York 10016.
BERKLEY and the "B" design are trademarks of
Berkley Publishing Corporation.

PRINTED IN THE UNITED STATES OF AMERICA

10 9 8 7 6 5 4 3

CONTENTS

Introduction   vii

1. WILL THE REAL DOG PLEASE SIT UP   1

2. THE CANINE RESPONSE   15

3. THE DOG THE PUPPY WILL BECOME   46

4. A DOG IN THE FAMILY   68

5. GETTING YOUR DOG UNDER CONTROL   104

6. HOUSE TRAINING YOUR DOG   144

7. MISBEHAVIOR   161

8. THE AMERICAN KENNEL CLUB'S
    "CANINE GOOD CITIZEN TEST"   213

INTRODUCTION

This book is about living with the best dog possible. But what is the best dog? Is it the clip-and-comb glamour hound of the blue-ribbon set? The eat-and-sleep couch coyote? The scruffy scamp running with a bunch of kids in a TV movie? Some people think that famous dogs are the best ones. It's easy to confuse show business with reality and fall in love with Snoopy, Lassie, or Benji. But how practical is that? Snoopy is made of newsprint and video tape. He's only a cartoon and continues to outlive many generations of real dogs. Lassie was a fictional character played by as many as twenty different Collies. Benji was also a fictional creation played by several method-acting dogs, both male and female. *Say it ain't so*. So which are the best dogs? The answer has nothing to do with being a show dog, a house dog, a fictional or nonfictional dog. The best dogs are the ones who please you the most, and that has a lot to do with behavior and misbehavior.

Your dog's behavior is the most important aspect of a successful pet relationship. The natural behavior of dogs is compatible, for the most part, with the way humans live if it is understood and dealt with properly. For example, dogs are highly social animals and will develop a deep and lasting relationship with humans if given the chance. It is this quality that makes them so endearing.

Understanding natural dog behavior helps dog owners cope with housebreaking problems, chewing, barking, and all the other upsetting things that dogs like to do. Learning what goes on inside your dog's mind will help to create the bond that is so desirable between humans and their pets. Once the bond is established, new dogs become members of the family and bring out a loving instinct that makes most new dog owners parents, pals, or partners.

Because we feel so deeply about our dogs, we tend to think of them as humans. We interpret their every move as human behavior rather than dog behavior, from panting tongues to quivering tails. All pet owners are like this, from presidents to movie stars to everyone who ever showed off photos of the family pet. The fact is, however, that there is such a thing as *natural* dog behavior and it is quite different from *human* behavior. If you understand the difference, you can prevent many behavioral problems from developing and manage most of those that are already present. All dogs, no matter how they live with humans, are born with a set of natural behavior patterns that are exclusively canine. Some of them blend in perfectly with ours and some do not. This is true of house pets, show dogs, and every canine that ever crept into our hearts.

When considering the quality of dogs, one cannot ignore the distinctions between *pet owners* and *dog fanciers*. Although they often overlap, these two groups are involved with *Canis familiaris* in different ways. The differences are important.

Pet owners think of their dogs as members of the family. How they treat their dogs depends on how they treat their families. Pet dogs are expected to give and receive love and companionship in exchange for kind treatment, a full belly, and a warm place to sleep. Some pets are four-legged love objects and are smothered with affection, food, and constant attention. Some pets are treated like rich relatives. Their misbehavior is either ignored or regarded as endearing and is simply tolerated, no matter what. However, the typical family dog risks losing the love of his family when his behavior becomes unacceptable or unbearable. Most pet dogs cannot escape the consequences of their own unacceptable behavior unless their human benefactors learn how to change it or cope with it.

Dog fanciers, on the other hand, have a professional interest and expect more than companionship and member-of-the-family status. They are the breeders, exhibitors, handlers, show judges, veterinarians, professional groomers, writers, and connoisseurs of the canine arts, sciences, and sports. Although many dog fanciers relate to their dogs as pets, they are concerned with every aspect of the dog world, including professional health care, competition in the various dog sports, and breed preservation.

Serious dog fanciers, especially breeders, judges, and handlers are, in a practical sense, historians and stewards of the many dog breeds that exist today. They are part of an effort to preserve (and possibly improve) the best physical and mental qualities of the various dog breeds. They help to create and preserve breed standards by which individual dogs are measured for their look, temperament, and function. The principles of genetics, animal husbandry, and good dog handling are necessary to achieve their goals.

Pure-bred dogs must be carefully selected for their best characteristics before they are allowed to mate. They must measure up to the standard created for their respective breeds. Temperamentally unstable, physically impaired, or seriously flawed examples of a breed are usually rejected for breeding by conscientious dog fanciers. The goal of very serious breeders is to produce healthy puppies that grow into beautiful dogs. Their dogs must represent the "standard" of their breeds as set forth by a national breed club and adopted by the American Kennel Club, the United Kennel Club, or some other national dog organization that registers pure-bred dogs. As you can see, the differences between dog fanciers and pet owners are great.

Unless you want to compete at dog shows or begin a serious breeding program, your dog's "papers," AKC or otherwise, have no value except to keep the floor clean. It is not important if your dog is a pure-breed or a mixed-breed, a movie star or a dog-on-the-street. The most important consideration is that your dog is compatible with you, enjoyable, and under control. The best dogs for pet owners are not necessarily Champions of Record or blue ribbon winners. The best dogs are the ones that are healthy, happy, easy to love, who have entered your lives and altered your capacity for change while teaching you something about your feelings.

This book is about understanding dogs, and how to make life better for them and the people who love them. It deals with what is acceptable and unacceptable dog behavior, and realistic and unrealistic human expectations. It is a practical book presenting some solutions to some problems by offering an informal understanding of why dogs are the way they are.

WILL
THE REAL DOG
PLEASE SIT UP

Dogs only *seem* like people. But dogs are dogs. It is important to understand this. Dog behavior pertains only to dogs and other canines. Human behavior pertains only to humans, even though there are similarities between the two. We are compatible with our pets because of those similarities. However, human psychology is of no help to a dog owner trying to understand his or her pet's good or bad behavior. It's like comparing a chocolate cake to a box of dog biscuits. The only connection between "dog psychology" and "human psychology" is the emotional response pets create in us.

Emotions

Yes, dogs have emotions but not in the same way as humans, whose feelings are influenced by complicated mental activity. When dogs experience pleasant feelings they are triggered by real events happening directly to them in the present moment. They may involve food, play, companionship, or any immediate form of sensual gratification.

Human beings may experience pleasant emotions in the same way, but they are also capable of having good and bad feelings from their thoughts. For better or worse, human emotions often come from abstract thoughts or from the imagination. Dogs do not show much evidence of this form of mental activity. That is probably why dogs are easier to understand than people.

It does not take a rocket scientist to recognize a happy dog. Nor does it require a genius to know when a dog is content with his family and is enjoying a good life.

Of course, dogs also experience the unpleasant emotions of anxiety, fear, depression, and anger. These are brought about as a direct response to something that is happening in the immediate sense, or as a response to a need or desire that is being denied. However, emotions are also created by associations. Dogs that have been hit in the past, for example, may become fearful and cringe if anyone raises their arms over them. Something or someone that reminds them of an intense experience may elicit a powerful emotional response. Of course, some dogs are born with inherited shyness, fearfulness, anxiety, etc., and exhibit such behavior with little or no justification.

An understanding of your dog's emotions as they pertain to his natural canine behavior not only helps you develop a good relationship with him but also can be helpful in preventing or solving problem behavior. Quite often a dog may display one or more behavioral problems that cannot be solved no matter what the owner tries. This complicated situation may be the result of failing to recognize the underlying problem. For example, excessive barking, housebreaking failures, or destructive behavior could all be caused by *separation anxiety*, a condition having to do with stress brought about by being left alone. By coping with the dog's separation anxiety, you will probably be more successful with his other behavioral problems, which are merely the result of his condition rather than distinct problems themselves.

The solutions to the behavioral problems of dogs are as different as one dog is from another. There are no pat answers. What works for one dog may not work for another. The same problem may have to be solved in ten different ways for ten different dogs. Inexperienced pet owners might as well throw away preconceived ideas and advice from amateurs. So what are they supposed to do? They must acquaint themselves with the basics of dog behavior, use the various obedience-training and problem-solving techniques that are known to have worked with some dogs, and also become sensitive to their dogs' emotions as they pertain to natural canine behavior. Assuming the relationship with your dog is important, the solution for an emotional problem requires human effort and understanding. You must be able to evaluate your dog's behavior as being normal or abnormal—*for a dog*.

Neurosis

The neurotic dog is as American a concept as apple pie with a tail on it. Our popular culture has enthusiastically embraced the idea of a maladjusted, hypersensitive, self-destructive, compulsive-obsessive, manic-depressive dog. All that's missing from this notion is chain-smoking and sleeping pills. Is there really such a thing as a neurotic dog?

If your dog were to whisper in your ear that he is depressed, anxiety-ridden, self-doubting, guilt-ridden, lonely, cynical, alienated, and unable to sustain a meaningful relationship, then it could be said that he *might* be neurotic. *Neurosis*, however, is a medical term describing a *human* emotional disorder caused by unresolved conflicts, with anxiety its primary characteristic. It is a word meant to describe a pattern of human traits and emotions. However, many people cannot wait to tell anyone who will listen the latest horror story about their dog. "My dog is so neurotic he punishes me whenever I leave him alone by dumping on my bed. The dog is sick."

The truth is that such stories pertain to dogs with *problems* rather than *neuroses*. It would be more useful to avoid the term "neurotic" when attempting to describe problematic behavior in dogs. Dogs often find themselves in a situation that stimulates them into behaving exactly as they were intended. When this happens it may upset the human family. An anxiety-ridden dog leaves messages by defecating or urinating over the scent-posted area of the pack leader. The bed sheets are perfect for this, from the dog's perspective. It is important to understand that housebreaking and other forms of training demands are imposed rules meant to satisfy humans, and have nothing to do with a dog's natural inclinations.

In fairness to pet owners, one must recognize that some behavior problems represent unnatural behavior and can be loosely defined as neurotic. Phobias such as fear of heights, fear of thunder, fear of strangers, or unusually aggressive behavior should be considered abnormal. Even here, those who train dogs, as well as professional dog behaviorists, resist using the word "neurotic." Most professional dog trainers refer to these behaviors as *dog problems* and deal with them in a practical manner. They do not attempt to make a dog non-neurotic.

Is a dog neurotic if he obeys every impulse that is true to his canine instincts? It is not reasonable to expect a dog to behave differently just because the human demands of home life clash with natural canine behavior. All dogs have been genetically programmed by nature to behave in certain ways under certain conditions. For example, dogs are instinctively drawn to a group resembling a pack. In our homes the human family substitutes for this pack. Dogs develop territories (in your home, usually), establish ranking order within their pack, defend their territory, and fight to establish a rank in the pecking order (to the death, in some instances). These traits are especially strong in male dogs. It is normal. These are the instincts that are at work in most cases involving aggressive dogs. Whether aggressiveness is a problem or not depends on what the human family expects from their dog. Some families want a dog that will aggressively protect them, while other humans are simply more tolerant of negative behavior. Extremely aggressive dogs may be expressing a medical problem, or their behavior may be the result of early abuse. The same can be true of a shy or nervous dog. Also, a dog may inherit these qualities from its parents or may simply possess exaggerated aspects of its breed characteristics. The problem is often solved by firmly establishing a subordinate attitude in the dog and a dominant attitude in the owner. Dog trainers can be helpful with this.

When we look at a dog barking uncontrollably or behaving in a frantic manner, it is most certainly an animal in stress. The animal is preparing for some form of action and may fight, take flight, or simply express his agitation in some destructive or upsetting manner.

Stress involves the nervous system, which precipitates chemical changes so that the order of priorities are altered within the body. The heart pumps faster, the blood pressure rises, sending oxygen to the skeletal muscles instead of the skin, intestinal system, and the kidneys. If stress continues over a prolonged period of time, the physiology of the animal's body is harmed, sometimes seriously. Violations of the animal's needs will cause stress, which in turn will either intensify the situation or add new and even more extreme behavior.

For this reason it is important to discover what it is that upsets the dog and causes the extreme behavior. In many cases, something in the dog's environment is disturbing the animal. This could range from a simple telephone ring that is frightening, or a child that grows bigger and thus threatens the dog's position of dominance in the pack structure. Obviously, abusive or inhumane treatment will alter a dog's behavior. A death in the family, divorce, a child going off to school for the first time, even a stranger entering your property are all events that can create an emotional response that causes stress to the dog's nervous system. Boredom and loneliness, however, are the two greatest negative factors in creating stress and the resulting problem behavior in dogs.

The most common forms of canine problem behavior fall into the following categories: housebreaking failures; aggressiveness (threatening, biting, attacking); failure to obey humans; nervousness (barking, digging, chewing, jumping, or running away); fear responses (cringing, hiding, shaking, nipping, wetting, chewing, barking); and phobias (fear of confinement, isolation, thunder, strangers, outdoors). No doubt many dog owners can add to this list. There is no common cure that works every time for all of these problems. As in human therapy, each dog must be treated individually according to the demands of his personality, problem, and environmental situation. However, there are guidelines and a few basic suggestions that can be useful.

First, it is important to reassure your pet that he is loved and in no danger of losing his home. A loving home with hands-on affection plus individual attention based on your pet's needs will lay a solid foundation for solving behavioral problems. Next, firmly and unwaveringly establish all humans as dominant members of the pack (family), and the dog as the subordinate member. Look for environmental factors that may be upsetting the dog and try to correct them. If appropriate, take such practical measures as lowering the sound of the phone or not leaving the animal alone for long periods. Sometimes simply being patient, showing affection, and implementing a gentle approach to dog training are the most effective techniques for solving canine behavioral problems.

Depending on the problem and its severity, you may hire a dog trainer or an animal behaviorist specializing in behavioral problems. It is best to seek out an animal behaviorist with a veterinary degree or a background in dog training. Some veterinarians work with behaviorists and will be able to recommend one. Experience has proven, however, that a skilled and talented dog trainer can be more effective in solving problem behavior, providing he or she uses nonabusive techniques.

Bear in mind that human neurosis may be characterized as a disorder of the personality in which behavior is defensive and often extreme. The neurotic person experiences anxiety because of unconscious efforts to solve unconscious conflicts. This may create loss of memory, obsessions, compulsions, hysteria, phobias, imagined (or real) illnesses, and depression. Subtlety and imagination make human neurosis enigmatic and elusive. Canine behavior is exquisitely clear in its abnormal state. Canine neurosis can be so clear that you often feel its bite. When you do, try to figure it out and then look for help.

Expectations

Most pet owners think of their dogs as the most loyal members of their families who never grow up, never leave home, and never forget to write. For some, they are the children they never had (or wanted). This often leads to confusion about the animals they live with. Dogs are *not* furry humans with tails. The more we understand about our pets, the happier we can make them which, in turn, makes us happier.

For example, all dogs are not necessarily canine versions of Arnold Schwarzenegger and obedience training is not a violation of their nature. If they could speak, they would tell you about themselves and what they are really like.

Puppy Report Card

Do you remember the story on "60 Minutes" about the trend to create super babies? They showed infants and toddlers (still trying to get oatmeal on a spoon) being taught art, poetry, higher mathematics, and science. The glaze in the children's eyes and their smirking faces seemed to indicate that they would prefer to have their diapers changed and be allowed to run off and play. Unfortunately, there is a similar trend to make every little dog a *phi beta puppy*. When it comes to puppies it is all too easy to create serious behavioral problems by introducing sophisticated teaching methods and then expecting too much, too soon.

As there are overly ambitious parents, there are also overly ambitious dog owners. The burden of great expectations are placed on the little shoulders of dogs as young as three months. There is no question that these dog owners have only the best intentions. Training dogs and adapting them to human lifestyles and needs is highly desirable, and can only help to secure a place in the hearts and homes of novice dog owners. But overzealous puppy parents can do more harm than good.

Behavioral patterns in dogs develop early. What happens to a dog in a new home the first weeks has a profound influence on his behavior for the rest of his life. Five-week-old puppies tend to imitate those that are around them the most: mother dog, and the litter mates. It is the beginning of learned behavior, as opposed to behavior that develops instinctively. Puppies tend to imitate our attitudes and emotional and physical actions. The way a human relates to his or her dog the first few weeks that they're together helps determine the dog's behavioral patterns, and may play a role in shaping the animal's temperament.

When you live with a new dog, there is one essential that must come before training commands, or even housebreaking. It is *bonding*. The term refers to the growth of an emotional tie between the family pet and everyone living with him. A new dog, young or old, must feel that he belongs, that he is a part of the family. Once the dog has been exposed to human contact during the earliest phase of puppyhood, his desire to become part of the human family is very powerful.

Bonding is the emergence of strong emotions, positive mental attitudes, and a protective concern toward another person or living creature. It is a natural condition between parents and children, and between humans and their pets. An established emotional bond is the essential catalyst that compels us to do the right thing for those who are vulnerable and in need of nurturing and protection. Part of the ritual of natural childbirth is to hand the newborn baby to the mother and father immediately after delivery. Between the last contraction and the first hug arise emotions between parents and child that endure for a lifetime. They establish "the bond." Tender handling of a puppy has the same good effect. A demanding, overpowering manner, introducing adult-style dog training, and expecting too much, too soon from a puppy can obstruct or even prevent the bonding process. The potential for a loving, joyful relationship may wane under such conditions and with it the possibility for fifteen years of pleasurable companionship.

Never Spoil Your Puppy

This is one of the more recent myths of dog ownership. It is simply not correct. That you must constantly discipline a puppy and never let him get away with anything is a popular misconception. Expect puppies to do most things wrong, in the beginning. It is our responsibility to educate ourselves so that the appropriate methods are used to teach as we nurture a little dog.

Maturity for most dogs is achieved at the end of the first year of life. (Giant breeds mature a little later.) Typically, puppies are taken to their new homes between two and three months of age. Try to compare a three-to-five-month-old puppy with a kindergarten child; a five-to-seven-month-old dog with a juvenile; a seven-to-twelve-month-old dog with a teenager.

How much would you expect from a child in nursery school or even kindergarten? How much *can* you expect? It almost answers itself. Do not misunderstand. This is an important time for puppies as well as children. Rules must be established, but they are more like guidelines and general boundaries in the beginning. Puppies must negotiate a learning process before we can expect them to behave like obedient angels. The learning process must be neither harsh nor unforgiving. A firm, demanding approach to training comes later, usually in the sixth month, depending on the breed and individual dog.

Smart Dog—Dumb Dog

Which dog breeds are the most intelligent? This always
leads to a hot debate. Dogs probably want their families
to understand that humans should understand the difference
between trainability, performance, and intelligence. There
is no evidence that one breed of dog is more intelligent than
another. Most breeds were developed by humans exercising
genetic selection to perform one or more specific tasks,
making some breeds more adept at performing certain tasks
than another. It is not a matter of intelligence.

For example, German Shepherd Dogs make superb guard
dogs. Labrador Retrievers are excellent guide dogs for the
blind (in addition to retrieving for bird hunters). Border
Collies herd sheep better than any other breed. There are
at least four hundred dog breeds throughout the world and
they were all developed to excel at one thing or another.

Still, some breeds are easier to train than others. This,
however, is not necessarily because of the animal's intelligence. It has to do with faster or slower mental processes,
temperament variations, and the dog's willingness to accept
the various degrees of human dominance. In some cases,
poor trainability may indicate greater intelligence.

Mongrel Versus Pure-Breed

The question of which is better to own, a mongrel or a pure-
bred dog, can lead to angry arguments. The answer depends
on whom you ask and what you mean by better. Mongrels
cost less money, are easier to get, and are as lovable as
any expensive pure-bred dog. You probably wouldn't give
a very expensive show dog to a child, but a mongrel puppy

is almost always ideal. When properly cared for, they are as healthy as pure-bred dogs and enjoy the same life span as pure-breeds of comparable size and type.

The primary advantage to owning a pure-bred dog is its predictability of physical appearance and, to some degree, of temperament. Another advantage is the ability to breed and show pure-bred dogs. You cannot enter a mongrel in an American Kennel Club or United Kennel Club dog show. But you can never be accused of being snobbish with a mongrel. If you acquire a mongrel from a pound or shelter you can pat yourself on the back and say, "I am a kind, humane person. I saved a dog's life."

Introductions

The first moment you walk into your home with a new puppy or dog has an influence on things to come. When first entering your house with a new puppy, the objective is to complete the disturbing transition for the dog with as little trauma and over-stimulation as possible. It is certainly impossible to bring a puppy into a house where children live and deprive them of meeting the new members of the family. This applies to the adult residents as well. In order to satisfy this urgent need, you may offer a quick but gratifying peek. Devote five minutes for quick introductions and one or two *calm* pats on the dog's head. Make it clear that the family—especially the children—are not to stimulate the dog with loud squeals, giggles, hugs, kisses, or other physicalized or overly-vocalized expressions of delight. Remember, it's the dog we are concerned with at this point. After the brief time allotted for introductions, chase the family into another part of the house for at least an hour and perhaps the rest of the day.

Noise

By prior arrangement with the family, keep the noise level to a bare minimum. Loud sounds interfere with the puppy's ability to accept the new environment as his own. Obviously, a high-pitched phonograph or television, or the squeals of children at play will scare some puppies. It will be more difficult for him to adjust to your home and to his new "pack." The same would be done for a human infant first entering his home from the hospital. Peace and quiet, low-key lighting, and contained enthusiasm in the first hour help relax and reassure a new puppy.

Do not be discouraged by those who advocate the "harsh realities of a dog's life" philosophy. They are either uninformed or living with dogs on a basis other than that of companionship and member-of-the-family status. You may also find yourself criticized by those who do not wish to make this much of an effort or emotional investment in your dog. That's fine—for them. It is not wrong to make every effort possible to create a long-lasting, pleasurable relationship with your dog. The "treat a dog like an animal" idea does not stand up against the reality that we, too, are animals, and that human contact with a dog demands humane considerations in that dog/human relationship. Even theories of child rearing conflict with one another and set off heated debates in the scientific-medical community, as well as among parents faced with the actual responsibility. Like a new parent, you will have to do what you think is best for yourself and your dog and then stick to it, no matter what anyone else says about it.

A Friendly Voice

It is absolutely impossible to predict how a new dog in your house will feel when he first arrives. It depends on his breed, the way he's been handled in the first eight weeks of his life, and many other variables. He may have been quite frisky when you got him but is now wilted or dejected from the great change. The most sensible goal for the new owner is to gain the dog's confidence. You have already begun if you kept the introductions short, lowered the noise level in the house, subdued the lighting, and not forced the dog to relate to anyone other than yourself. This raises the question of how to relate to the dog so that he will trust you and his new surroundings.

It has to do with communication. Everything you do or say has an effect on the dog. Ideally, you want to do and say those things that communicate safety, affection, and comfort to the baby dog. This is accomplished by avoiding sudden moves around the puppy, especially those motions that are directed at him. Move slowly and smoothly and do not grab or clutch. Although most dogs come to understand some words, they don't at this stage of puppyhood. Your puppy will respond positively to a soothing, gentle tone of voice. Do not be inhibited about talking to your dog. You will eventually talk to him anyway. You may experience direct communication at this early point if you start talking in a soft, friendly manner. Once you gain a dog's confidence, you will have it all his life . . . providing you don't abuse him. Having a dog's confidence means you will have little difficulty in shaping him into the kind of creature you want.

2

THE CANINE RESPONSE

Understanding the canine response to your dog's environment and to those in it is a major step toward developing a great relationship with him. It will also help you understand the differences and the similarities between humans and dogs.

The key to living happily with a dog is getting along with him. It is so easy to enjoy your dog once you have bonded with him and gotten him under control. This involves developing a loving relationship, obedience training, and learning to cope with behavioral problems such as barking, nipping, housebreaking mistakes, and all the other annoying and inconvenient behaviors.

These things are not difficult to accomplish if the new dog owner learns the actions and reactions of the basic dog, which are uncomplicated and simple to grasp. This fundamental information will help you appreciate your dog and understand why he does what he does. If you love your dog it is the most important thing to learn.

Canine behavioral responses are distinctive and similar to only a few species. Your pet's behavior becomes somewhat easier to interpret once you understand that dogs, wolves, and other species of the *Canidae* family behave similarly. It is fascinating to learn that some aspects of canine behavior parallel human behavior in terms of the need for social order and the avoidance of being alone. The similar needs and responses of dogs and humans are obvious. In a general sense, the habits and reactions of all animals are mostly predictable and based on what is understood about each species' *natural* behavior. What is not predictable is behavior that is genetically modified and spontaneously mutated or altered by environmental influences, such as abusive handling at an early age.

Your dog's *predictable* behavior has been established by nature long before he ever saw his mother, his litter mates, or his human family. The canine response to his environment is common to all doglike species such as the wolf, jackal, fox, coyote, and the various species of wild dogs. It is comprised of instinctive behaviors that are inherited by all members of the *Canidae* family. (It is important to understand, however, that there are behavior variations between each of these species.) Because all dogs and doglike species are meat eaters they must behave in a similar fashion if they are to survive in their wild environment. To best understand your dog you must first understand the way in which he would survive if he were on his own like his wild cousins. These survival behaviors have been evolving over the past fifty-five million years and can still be seen in the domestic dog, in a gentler, milder form.

Domestic dogs behave with fundamental similarities whether they live in comfortable homes in the city, on their own and eating out of garbage cans, or wandering in the forest as part of a free-roaming pack. It is their genetic destiny to behave in specific ways pertaining to survival and procreation. Canine behavior has been understandably modified to a great extent after thousands of generations of domesticity. Still, beneath the exterior of the gentle, loving dog is a clever hunter capable of bringing down animals much larger and stronger than himself with a tenacious ferocity that would surprise the average pet owner. *The domestic dog has descended from the wolf and that simple fact is the key to understanding the canine response.*

For many decades researchers have been observing wolves in natural habitats and in artificially created environments and have carefully recorded their data. What is understood about wolves has been of enormous significance in understanding the behavior of dogs, partly by inference and partly by formal research. This is why dog behavior is so well understood, which ironically, has not been studied seriously until very recently. The similarities between pet dogs and wolves living in a free, natural environment have to do with their instinct to live in group structures known as packs. With the wolf or dog pack the various members become bonded to each other in a social hierarchy for the purpose of survival and procreation. Every pack requires an alpha wolf (or dog) that is the most aggressive of the group. He (sometimes *she*) is the leader of the pack. The business of the pack is to find and hold a territory in which to live and hunt. Within their territory a den is established where they sleep and, more or less, live in privacy. A large, outer range is that portion of the territory where they roam in search of animals to hunt for food. During the warm months of the year wolves remain within their fixed territory and eat squirrels, rabbits, small rodents, birds, fish, berries, and small fruits. However, as the weather turns cold they travel far beyond the boundaries of their territory, become nomadic, and follow the grazing herds (if available) as a source of food.

The distinction between domestic dog behavior and wolf behavior is more a matter of adaptation and intensity than actual difference. The two species both live in packs, require living in a social structure based on rank, and will defend their territories from other packs or individual non-pack members.

Domestic dogs are far more adaptive to humans, cats, and other non-dogs than wolves and are less intense about changes in their environment. Dogs are also more trusting than wolves. A wolf's reaction to intrusion is usually the *fight or flight* response. Most dogs in that situation take their cue from the human family's behavior which is the result of living as a companion animal.

Nevertheless, domestic dog behavior is simply a modified version of the untamed behavior that is so necessary for survival in the wild state. For example, the leader of a wolf pack is, by necessity, an aggressive animal that can be ferocious in the assertion of its dictates to the lower ranking wolves. A diluted version of this behavior can be seen in some aggressive house dogs. *Mistakenly, some pet owners dominate their dogs in the harsh, overbearing manner of a wolf-pack leader resulting in the creation of a fearful, shy, or aggressive dog. A dog that fears you is not a good companion and makes an undesirable pet.*

There is a consensus of opinion that the domestic dog evolved from the wolf. Despite the incredible differences between dogs and dog breeds in size, shape, coat type, temperaments, skills and degrees of sociability, they all belong to the same species, *Canis familiaris* (the domestic dog). Strange but true, both St. Bernard and Chihuahua are members of the same species as are all dog breeds.

The physical and mental differences in dogs and dog breeds are the result of an evolutionary response to extreme weather conditions, variations of terrain, environmental demands, and the availability of food. However, many dog breeds look and behave they way they do because of human intervention in the breeding process. With the understanding of genetics and animal husbandry dog breeders have been able to emphasize or de-emphasize specific physical or mental qualities in the breed of their choice. This has been done over the centuries to develop various breeds for specific purposes such as herding sheep or pulling sleds. Nevertheless, the canine response to its environment is basically the same in all dog breeds and is a modified version of wolf behavior.

Dog behavior is based on the following fundamental factors: Wolves, wild dogs, and domestic dogs are social animals who instinctively live in groups known as packs. Members of the pack bond to each other. A pack leader always emerges, most often a male, and is the most aggressive of the group with keen leadership qualities. A wolf or dog pack requires a territory in which to live and hunt. Survival is based on the pack's ability to find and catch prey animals for food. Dogs have an overpowering instinct to mate, whelp puppies, nurture and protect them until they are old enough to survive on their own.

The Pack

Dogs, like wolves, are animals that live in a pack or communal structure which is the essence of their nature. The pack can be likened to a nation that works together and strives to make life safe and prosperous for all its citizens. But in order to achieve those goals everyone must play a part and serve some function. Within the pack a social order develops, based on strength, courage and leadership abilities. The establishment of the social order is an ever-changing process with many challenges and reassertions of rank. The business of the pack is to hold on to its territory, hunt for prey animals and secure them as food by bringing down the strays, the old, and the dying members of grazing herds.

Mating takes place, cubs or pups are born, and they are nurtured, fed, and protected. The pack replenishes itself with new population once a year and life goes on. This all happens within the discipline of a rigid social strata. When the leader can no longer defend his rank he is deposed and replaced with another, usually younger and stronger, wolf. A sick or wounded member of the pack is treated like one that loses its rank. It is either killed or abandoned for the sake of the survival of the pack.

A wolf pack or wild-dog pack is only as large as the territory that can sustain it. Every member must pull his or her weight and take an earned place in the social structure.

Despite the fact that domestic dogs never live with these conditions, and despite the fact that domesticity has brought them very far from such a stark lifestyle, they nevertheless possess all the fundamental behaviors of the canine response. It is their behavioral heritage. All dogs have such genetically organized traits and even the gentlest house pet inherits these behaviors and responses.

The pet dog uses the human family as a substitute for the pack structure. This is true even if the family consists of only one dog and one human. The need to live socially with others is one of the great behavioral similarities between dogs and people. It is the primary reason that dogs live so successfully with humans. Another important reason for this success is that dogs accept a subordinate position when humans take a dominant position. It is an interesting phenomenon when the dog takes the dominant role and the human takes the subordinate role as it occasionally happens in the pet/family configuration. Once the order of rank has been established, it is extremely difficult to change it without upsetting everyone.

The romantic notion of the "lone wolf" is an idea created in works of fiction and has no basis in natural dog behavior. Many animals, including some humans, pack animals, and herding animals, will die in the face of plenty if they lose their positions in their respective societies. There is strong evidence that all animals are either given or develop a role for themselves in their social framework. When an animal is denied that role because of failing health, defeat, or alienation, he becomes a 'lone wolf' because the pack has rejected his presence and is sentenced to an isolated existence. The so-called lone wolf is forced to wander off on a meaningless journey from which there is no return.

It is almost impossible for a lone wolf to hunt for food. Only by working as a group can a pack find and capture a large animal such as a caribou, a moose, or even a deer. Dogs and wolves living in a pack develop all of the skills needed for hunting which include scenting and sighting the prey; strategically herding prey animals into a vulnerable position; unleashing the aggression necessary to bring down the prey and kill it. These skills are developed for a specialized purpose at the expense of all the other skills. Tracking by scent or sight, herding, attacking, and guarding skills are essentially part of pack behavior. Veterinarians like to say that members of a free-roaming pack can be viewed as *general practitioners* while dogs of a given breed, such as Huskies or Collies, can be thought of as *specialists*.

Dogs or wolves that do not belong to a specific pack are driven off when they attempt to attach themselves to an established group. They are not tolerated and are usually attacked when they approach. There are diluted versions of this behavior in the domestic dog, especially in some of the more territorial breeds such as the Rottweiler, the German Shepherd Dog, and various other breeds. The working and herding breeds are the most territorial and will defend their territories and protect their families and property by chasing away or attacking dogs or humans that they view as intruders. The human family is the ideal substitute for the dog pack and is the behavioral link between people and their pets.

Social Attachments

There are various forms of social attachments that free-living wolves and other wild *canids* form. The most interesting of these is the "pair bond." This is the formation of a relationship between a male and a female that comes about out of the instinct to mate, to reproduce, and to nurture the offspring until they become adults. It is in this area of sexual behavior that wild *canids* differ from domestic dogs.

Male wolves and coyotes are essentially monogamous and mate with one female for life. Female wolves experience one estrous cycle a year. Female dogs experience at least two. Occasionally, a wolf pack leader does not mate. In such instances, he leaves the business of breeding to lower ranking males who also form pair bonds and mate exclusively with one female. However, a male dog on the loose will mount any wandering female in heat. The instinct to pair bond does exist in dogs but in non-sexual terms. Pet dogs will undoubtedly form exclusive, emotional attachments to one or more humans, to another dog, or even to a cat who they accept as a member of their pack.

The reason we are able to establish emotional ties with pet dogs is because of their need to be with other creatures and their predispostion to develop close relationships. Domestic dogs living as pets shift their instinct to bond from dogs to humans, providing their experiences with humans have been positive.

Pack survival requires a well-developed social structure within the group. The order of rank and the acceptance of various responsibilities enable the pack to maintain a territory, hunt (which is a group effort) and extend the life of the pack through sexual reproduction.

All dogs are social creatures because of their instinct to live in a pack. As stated before, the pack is essentially a small family of *canids* living together in a very specific social organization. If your dog is left alone most of the time, as some pets are, he is living out an existence without the social attachments and activities that are so essential to his mental stability. It is similar to the unhappy state of the lone wolf. Isolation is unnatural for a dog. A lone wolf is one who has become too old or too sick to fulfill his destiny within the pack order. He becomes an outcast and does not last long in the remote wilderness because he has lost his social attachments. All aspects of life within the pack, which include the formation of social attachments, are the primary factors that promote mental and physical stability.

The Pack Leader

Few communities survive without a source of authority and the same is true for animals that live together. Nature has provided an instinct in every member of a wolf pack to accept the authority of a leader or to become a leader. In the social organization of wolves and wild dogs the leader of the pack is usually the most aggressive animal (usually a male), the most powerful, and the must cunning member of the group. The leader of the pack in most instances has taken the position by force of will and a ferocious fight for the job. Once the leader has been established the other members of the pack become dominant or subordinate based on the outcome of lesser conflicts. The results of those conflicts establish the order of rank within the pack. Although the method of choosing a leader is primitive, it is effective. The survival of the pack depends on a strong leader and nature has chosen the most efficient procedure for selecting one.

Once the job of leadership has been determined, and the members of the pack have established the pecking order, they all assume various tasks and privileges based on their rank. Hunting, mating, and establishing territory are the essentials for pack survival. These tasks are all accomplished by group effort.

The behaviors necessary for pack survival are present in dogs as well as wolves. Living as a pet does not alter this. A dog simply transfers the need for a leader to the human environment and adapts his pack behavior to the structure we call family. As in a pack, a dog will accept the authority of those in the family who behave in a dominant manner. When no one in the family is perceived by the dog as dominant he instinctively assumes the role of pack leader. From his point of view, a leader is essential and he will take that responsibility if no one else will. It is a matter of survival. Unfortunately, this makes dog training or solving behavior problems much more difficult to accomplish.

Potential pack leaders have aggressive qualities that are either inherited or influenced by the behavior of their littermates or by the events of the first months of life. These qualities can be seen in the nest as newborn cubs or puppies struggle to establish a teat for breast feeding. Once it is claimed, the teat becomes a personal possession or territory and aggressive puppies do not tolerate trespassers. By the second and third month play behavior becomes combative and assertive. By observing puppies in their litter one can see a microcosm of pack behavior with all of the rituals of establishing dominant and subordinate ranks. From twelve to sixteen weeks of age many displays of combat are seen in the litter as fights start and end quickly, resulting in the establishment of a dominant and subordinate position. After sixteen weeks personalities begin to take shape for the life of the dogs. Aggressive dogs tend to remain aggressive, shy dogs remain shy, and so on. The puppies' temperaments become set.

The leader of a wolf pack usually has a somber, menacing personality who commands with absolute authority and maintains his position with snarling threats to insubordinate members of the pack. He is dominant in all things. The leader is the first to eat after the hunt and is followed by those in the pecking order. Those who study wolves refer to him as the alpha wolf.

All members of the pack take their cue from the alpha wolf's reaction to anything out of the ordinary, such as intrusion of their territory. The alpha wolf leads the hunt, subdues his challengers, and tolerates nothing less than total submission from the pack. The assertion of dominance over another member of the pack is ritualized with body language. The pack leader stands straight, with his ears erect and his tail in a fixed, rigid position. He curls his lips upward, exposing his threatening teeth and growls. It is usually enough to subdue an offending lesser wolf who then assumes a stooped posture and flattens his or her ears as the tail lowers between the legs.

The dominant wolf or dog establishes his superiority by standing over the submissive one with his head over the other's neck and abdomen. This ritual avoids the need for fights to the death which would disrupt the normal life of the pack. Some pet dogs will display dominant behavior in their homes unless they are convinced that they are the subordinate members of the family. When pets are aggressive they are dangerous and undesirable as companion animals. Whenever a dog exhibits aggressive behavior he must be corrected immediately to prevent a potentially dangerous biting event.

Territory

The essence of a wolf or dog's existence is the territory it has staked out and claimed as its legitimate area for hunting, mating and sharing with its pack (or human family). The territory can be an area ranging from fifty to six hundred square miles, if the environment permits it. The number of pack members is often determined by how much prey there is in the territory to hunt. A sufficient number of deer, moose, caribou, etc. allows the pack to breed and whelp new cubs. This prevents the pack members from dying from lack of food.

An important aspect of the territory is the den which can be a cave, a series of hollow logs in a quiet, protected area, or simply some holes dug to provide a pregnant wolf a place to give birth. The den area becomes the hub of activity for the entire pack during the three or four months of pregnancy. The den is a safety area where the pack rests, eats, sleeps, and cares for the mother-to-be. It is also where the cubs will be nurtured during the most helpless period of their young lives. A dog living in the human environment also establishes territory. He may consider the outer perimeter of the house as his territory or he may consider the entire neighborhood to be his. The den may be the entire house, a room, a corner of a room, a dog bed or a wire dog crate.

Wolves seldom fight to defend the outer portions of their territory. It must be shared with many animals including other wolves. That is why overlapping territorial boundaries between wolf packs are tolerated. The dens, and other lairs, no matter how temporary are areas that can create fights to the death. These areas are protected vigorously and even the most casual intruder will be driven off. A dog living in the human environment may behave in a similar manner, depending on his breed and temperament. The place your dog rests is an element in his life that provides comfort and security. It is very important to him. Dogs feel best when enjoying the peace and comfort of the den.

Territory influences your dog's behavior in three ways:

1) Defense of territory. Dogs that are aggressive and territorial will become combative when a stranger approaches their territory. This could happen the minute the intruder sets foot on your property or upon entering your house. Getting near where the dog's food bowl is placed could set him off, as can coming too close to him while he is inside a parked car.

2) Claiming territory. This is accomplished by marking off the area with urine and feces. It is referred to as scent-posting. Another method of marking off territory is by scratching marks on the ground with the paws. This action is often seen immediately after eliminating and is mistaken by many as simply burying urine or feces. Quite often dogs will try to make visual marks with their paws even though they are on cement surfaces. Housebreaking dogs is accomplished by understanding this unique method of canine scent-posting and eliminating them inside the house and establishing them outside the house at specific locations.

3) The need for a den. A dog can become quite upset if he does not possess a den that belongs to him exclusively. You will avoid emotional stress by providing your dog with something that substitutes for a den. Within the house a metal dog crate (found at pet-supply stores or in pet catalogs) will serve well. Even a corner of the floor with a comfortable blanket or dog bed will do. Almost anything will work providing it belongs to the dog only and represents a place where he can sleep or get away from everyone without being disturbed. A dog's den is his sanctuary.

Hunting

Many hunting behaviors continue throughout the life of a pet dog despite the fact that he will never require them. All of their nutritional needs are taken care of by the family. In the domestic dog instinctive hunting behaviors can trigger upsetting responses to harmless events such as cars driving past your house, bikers and rollerbladers coasting by, running children, tossed balls, etc.

Wolf and wild dog packs hunt by tracking prey animals. This is accomplished by scent, sight or knowledge of the migrating trails of herd animals. Once the prey is found, various hunting strategies are used including splitting the pack into several smaller groups. One group chases the quarry as they run head on into another group. The hunters almost always separate one or more animals from the herd in order to bring it down without other animals from the herd being able to defend them. No matter how big the animal, it cannot defend itself from an entire wolf or dog pack. Even though hunting behaviors are necessary in the wild and irrelevent in domesticity, they can all be seen in pet dogs in one form or another. They are simply weaker versions of the same things, despite the fact that they seem to bear no relationship to hunting outside the context of pack behavior.

Specific dog breeds that have sheep and cattle herding skills are merely utilizing an aspect of pack hunting techniques. Dogs that serve as protection dogs are also employing behavior that appears in the hunt for food. Terriers that "go to ground" in pursuit of a badger, fox, or other tunneling animal is using its hunting instincts, of course. Breeds that assist bird hunters find the birds, point to their locations, and retrieve them after they have been shot. All of the hounds have been bred with an emphasis on either their keen sense of smell or their sense of sight. Gazehounds such as Greyhounds, Whippets, Afghans, Salukis, and others sight the prey with incredible accuracy and then swiftly outrun it.

Many dogs chase after cars driving past them. This problem behavior is not only dangerous for those concerned, it is also a source of trouble for the offending dogs' owners. Such dogs are the victims of their own hunting instincts which are triggered by the swift motion of a car. Dogs who do this have an emphasized hunting instinct which has no relationship to hunger, anger, or any apparant threat. Simply moving past the dog's line of sight elicits the response. In the human environment this is unacceptable behavior and must be dealt with as a serious problem.

The problem is extremely serious if the dog that chases also attacks what it can catch whether it is a cat, a mouse, a deer, or a person. Many states allow farmers and ranchers to shoot free-roaming dogs that chase and attack their livestock. Such dogs must be confined to their own property if they are to avoid being considered a menace to the community. Dogs that chase cars, animals, and people must not be allowed to roam free.

Mating

It is a natural part of a dog's life to mate and to reproduce, but every species in nature has been programmed to conform to its own unique set of behaviors and circumstances related to sexual activity. The sexual behavior of wild *canids* differs greatly from that of their domestic cousins. Wolves and coyotes are essentially monogamous and mate with one female for life. Female wolves experience one estrous cycle a year, while dogs experience two. In an extended pack the leader sometimes will not breed. In such cases, he will leave breeding to lower ranked males.

A male dog becomes sexually mature anywhere between six and eighteen months depending on the breed and the individual dog's physiology. The larger the breed, the longer it takes to reach maturity. The American Kennel Club does not register puppies unless both parents were at least one year old when mating. The female is considered mature when she has experienced her first estrous cycle, commonly referred to as "heat" or "being in season." Here again the breed and size of the dog affects maturity, which is reached between six and twelve months of age.

Because dogs have been domesticated for so many centuries, their sexual behavior varies greatly from the wolf
and other wild *canids*. Free-roaming dogs will breed indis-
criminately, but unless a dog has lived in a kennel or
pack situation, he has not had the opportunity to learn
proper sexual technique through observation. Confinement
and close contact with humans have somehow rendered
many male house pets hesitant and unassertive in breeding situations. This is not to say that a dog on the loose
will not successfully mount a wandering female in heat.
Many dogs must be guided and instructed during their
first mating. Some domesticated females become frenzied
in their first sexual encounter. This is not at all natural
to the dog, but is nonetheless common. Timing is also of
great importance. If a male is thrust into a situation with
a female who is not yet at the receptive moment of estrus,
she will behave in a very aggressive manner. This tends to
permanently affect the male's attitude toward mating if it
is his first experience.

It is customary to bring the female to the male on his
home ground. In the wild only the male claims territory.
There must be some time allowed for the two animals
to become acquainted through the wire of separate kennels, runs, or cages. The male should not be allowed to
eat two hours before mating, and both animals must be
toileted before being brought together. Noise, audience,
afternoon sun, and all forms of distraction must be avoided. Once the animals are introduced to each other they
can be left to perform sexually; however, they must be
observed to be certain that they have successfully mated.
Here, the knowledgeable breeder knows that assistance is
very often required, and knowing what to do and when
to do it comes from years of experience. Entire books

have been written on the subject of breeding dogs. It is important to understand the principles of pack behavior when it comes to sex between dogs. In a pack, a male is designated as leader because of his size, strength, courage, and ability to lead. He claims territory, finds prey, leads the others in making the kill, selects a mate and procreates with her. Even the most timid of domestic dogs bases his behavior on these principles. This is especially important when breeding dogs.

Breeding puppies for fun or profit is less than useless, it is ignorant and inhumane. If puppies are brought into the world for the benefit of a child's education, what is that child learning if the dogs end up being killed in a city dog pound or out on their own scavenging for food in garbage cans and in constant danger of being struck dead by a motor vehicle?

It is quite clear that male dogs do not have to breed in order to live full and happy lives. It is best never to introduce a male house dog to sex (arranged or otherwise) if he is not to function as a constant stud in a well-planned breeding program. The typical dog will not miss what he has never had and will in all probability not experience any frustration. For non-breeding male dogs the best and most humane thing a pet owner can do is take the dog to a veterinarian and have him neutered (castration). A castrated male dog is a wonderful pet that becomes sharply focused on his human family. It has been the experience of many dog owners that their male house dogs have had certain changes of personality after one or two matings. They can become more dominant, more territorial, less playful, less tolerant. This is not always the case but it remains a possibility and should be considered before allowing a house pet to breed.

The sexuality of the female is much different. Unless she is spayed (ovariohysterectomy), she will come into season twice a year and experience a hormonal and chemical change in her body at that time. A female usually experiences her estrous cycle every six months, and it normally lasts a total of twenty-one days. During the first week there is a bloody discharge which becomes somewhat colorless in the second week and disappears during the third and final week. This happens whether the dog is ever mated or not. During the three weeks of estrus, twice a year, it is necessary to confine the animal so that no males can get at her. If the dog is not going to be in dog shows or bred (as part of an intelligent breeding program), having her spayed early in life solves all problems pertaining to sex. Popular veterinary wisdom suggests that the sooner a female is spayed the less likely will she develop mammary tumors in later life.

For owners of unaltered dogs, both male and female, vigilance offers but one ounce of prevention. The full measure of prevention involves stemming the rising tide of unwanted pets by surgically neutering all dogs that are not part of a planned breeding program.

It takes nine weeks (sixty-three days) for a female dog to whelp a litter of puppies. This is an estimate because ovulation takes place approximately seventy-two hours before the end of receptivity. It takes three weeks for the fertilized egg to become implanted in the dog's uterus. When the puppies are born it is possible for them to be delivered up to twenty-four hours apart, although that is not common.

Maternal Behavior

Immediately after whelping a puppy the mother licks off the fetal membrane, ingests it, and severs the umbilical cord with her teeth. The neonatal puppy lies perfectly still until the mother licks its body, stimulating motion and sound from the newborn. At that point the pup begins to move about and faintly yelp. The pup is then either carried in the mother's mouth to a safe, warm place in the nest or must wait for more attention until the entire litter is whelped in much the same fashion. It is important to understand that puppies are born with a limited ability to move and no vision or hearing capability because their eyes and ears remain closed for approximately two weeks. With the exception of the sense of taste and touch, they are insulated from the outer environment. They can, however, crawl about slowly, moving their heads from side to side, in search of warmth, food, and the avoidance of pain, which are all provided by the mother dog.

The mother will nurse the puppies from the day of birth until approximately six weeks of age, with weaning beginning by the third week. There are usually three phases of nursing. The first phase begins at birth and lasts until approximately the end of the second week, during which the mother initiates the nursing of the puppies. The second phase begins in the third week and lasts for approximately seven days with both mother and puppies initiating nursing. The third phase begins in the beginning of the fourth week and lasts until the end of the fifth week, when the puppies initiate the nursing. By then the mother has begun weaning the pups away from breast milk and onto solid food. If humans do not intervene and provide solid food for the puppies, then the mother begins the weaning process herself as an instinctive behavior.

During the first three weeks of nursing it is normal for the mother to keep her nest free of puppy urine and feces. This behavior is possibly rooted in a natural inclination to avoid detection from predators. At this stage the puppies are not physically developed enough to eliminate their own body wastes without help. It is, therefore, accomplished through the efforts of the mother. The process of elimination is stimulated when the mother licks the puppies' stomachs and lower areas. She continues to lick them until they are clean of urine and feces. It is the only possible way to keep the nest free of waste matter. By three weeks of age, the puppies are able to stand, crawl, see, and hear. They begin to leave the nest independently and eliminate elsewhere.

This instinct to maintain a nest that is free of waste matter exists in most normal male and female dogs and has a significant impact on housebreaking, paper-training, and solving house soiling problems. A dog, or even a puppy, that is confined to one small area will try hard to avoid soiling it.

After the third week the mother leaves the nest for long periods, and when she returns she initiates the weaning process. She discourages the puppies from drawing milk from her teats and teaches them to eat solid food. This is accomplished by vomiting a recent meal into the nest, which is meant to be eaten by the litter. It is in this manner that puppies make the transition from breast milk to solid food. They eat with relish the meal that the mother provides, in addition to milk she makes available, and water given by humans. Weaning is a transitional process from milk to solid food that lasts from one to three weeks, depending on the size of the litter, the condition of the mother, and whether there is human help.

Play Behavior

Play behavior is an essential aspect of puppyhood. Like childhood, it is a time for mental and physical development aimed at preparing dogs for independence and self-sufficiency. It is essential to the survival of all dogs and the fulfillment of their destiny. Even though pet dogs have every need taken care of by their human families, nature still provides this learning process. When a litter of puppies or a single dog plays, it always has something to do with expending energy (exercise), learning how to fight (claiming territory, winning a mate, and confronting enemies), prey capture (hunting for food), or escape movements (survival). Puppies rarely hurt one another, even though they bite and chew as they roll and tumble with exuberance. However, a teething adolescent dog, bored and with a strong desire to play, can virtually destroy the home he lives in without meaning any harm.

At five months of age, a dog may give the appearance of being well on his way to maturity, but that is far from fact. For one thing, the dog's twenty-eight milk teeth are slowly being replaced by forty-two permanent ones. A youngster between four and seven months of age is in an intermittent state of teething. This can be a painful process, involving diarrhea, poor appetite, depression, listlessness, and an intense desire to chew. When a young dog is teething, he is invariably going to ease the pain by chewing on objects around the house. Easing the discomfort is accomplished by providing suitable chew toys made of digestible materials, ice cubes, or a moistened-then-frozen washcloth to help ease the pain.

By the eighth week of puppyhood most of the social development that began in the fourth week becomes much more pronounced, such as pack movement and antagonistic tendencies. Combative play becomes more intense as a means of developing the ranking order of dominance and subordination.

Mammals are more "playful" than other animals because of their longer childhood or interval of development. It is the time when their needs are taken care of by their parents and they have the luxury of time to learn the techniques for self-sufficiency and survival. The most important aspect of play behavior for dog owners to understand is its learning value for puppies. It is also, however, a useful promoter of exercise and physical fitness. To play is to pretend or "make believe." When a puppy plays, it is in the process of learning and then practicing what it has learned. When a child sits on the floor and manipulates a toy, one of two things is happening. Some new mental capacity is being developed, such as the ability to measure size and shape, or the child is practicing what he or she has seen his or her parents do in adult form, such as holding a telephone and speaking into it. When a puppy is on the floor playing he is learning behaviors for life in the wild that involve *prey capture*, *fighting*, or *escape behavior*. These are mechanisms of survival that would be necessary if he were to be on his own in a natural setting, such as the woods and forests from which he originally came. They are built in and preprogrammed. Nature could never have anticipated the domestication of dogs and the human desire to live with them as companion animals. And so, the puppy continues to learn how to survive through his instinct to play despite the fact that he will never even operate a can opener, let alone hunt for large game.

A PRACTICAL VIEW OF YOUR DOG'S FIRST YEAR OF LIFE

To understand a puppy is to understand the dog that he will become. As in human infancy, the early phases of a dog's life involve physical growth and mental development. Human childhood is a long stage, perhaps the longest in nature, and under the best circumstances involves two adult parents protecting, providing for, and instructing the child. Infancy to adulthood is compacted into one year in the life of a dog.

Birth to Three Months

The point to understanding this time in a puppy's life is to be able to produce a well-balanced dog that will adjust easily to humans and dogs. It is a time to develop a dog's capacity for a close dog/human bond. This capability is best developed between the third and twelfth week of a puppy's life. This is the time for the process of socialization which enables a dog to realize his maximum potential as a companion animal living in the human environment.

During these early weeks in your puppy's life, your job is simply to feed him, protect him from harm, handle him gently and affectionately, and, in a word, love him. It is a time to begin a little dog's housebreaking or paper training. You may even introduce the fundamentals of simple obedience training, but with sensitivity and gentleness. During this period it is most helpful to understand the critical periods of development.

The Critical Periods of Puppy Development

There are specific periods of time in a puppy's life when the slightest experience has the greatest impact on future behavior. These specific times are the "critical periods." They last for a short time and achieve the greatest effect on the dog the puppy will become. Few serious breeders in this country are unaware of the techniques of "socializing" and its importance during the critical periods of puppyhood. Understanding and implementing the process of "socialization" can make the difference between a great dog and a so-so dog. Here are the critical periods of canine development:

From Birth to the Thirteenth Day (Neonatal Period)

During this period the newborn puppy is completely dependent on its mother for everything. Its eyes and ears are closed and its ability to move about is restricted to a slow, forward motion. The puppy's nervous system is at a primitive stage of development and it cannot even maintain its own body temperature. It is the mother dog that provides milk, warmth and even the process of digestion through stimulation of the outer abdominal area with her tongue. There is no discernible learning during this period. Life for a neonatal pup consists of crawling about in search of warmth and nutrition.

The Thirteenth to the Twentieth Day (Transitional Period)

A rapid transformation begins at this time in the puppy's life. His eyes open and he begins to walk instead of crawl.

Exploration of the world beyond the mother's teat is the most notable change. At the end of this period the puppy is capable of leaving the nest for the purpose of independent urination and defecation. With the further development of the motor and sensory capacities, the little dog begins to interact with its environment. The tail begins to wag and the pup tries to satisfy its own needs. At the end of this period the ears open, allowing for responses to loud noises. At this stage it can also experience pain. On the twentieth day the teeth begin to erupt from the gums. The sleeping puppy is easily distinguished from the puppy that is awake. Almost all sensory and motor abilities are in place and functioning. The dog is about to enter a period of learning about creatures other than itself.

The Third Week to the Seventh Week

It is difficult to pinpoint the exact time when one phase ends and the next begins, but the times stated are very close approximations. Because the pup's sensory and motor capacities are not yet fully developed, he is still somewhat clumsy and uncoordinated. During this period the most important development is the beginning of social behavior. Over the next four weeks the brain and nervous system develop to the point of adult maturity. At the same time the puppy begins to socialize with its mother and litter mates. This canine socialization is extremely important. During this time the young dog learns to adjust to other dogs. Without the experience of this period, the dog will always be distrustful of other dogs and constantly pick fights with them as an adult.

At this time the process of weaning away from breast milk to whole food has begun, along with more sophisticated urination and defecation behavior. The areas used for this purpose become well-defined and farther from the nest. A sleeping puppy can refrain from eliminating for many hours. Also, puppies are learning to holler for help when they need it. If they are separated from the mother or other litter mates, they will cause a racket. Play and play-fighting with litter mates is apparent, along with intense investigatory behavior. The puppy will respond to the sight or sound of people or other animals with tail-wagging enthusiasm.

Up until this period the puppies engage in independent movement. But after the fourth week they begin to follow each other around, and by five weeks move together as a group. It is the beginning of pack behavior as adults.

By the seventh week weaning is complete. The mother refuses the puppies access to her breasts and threatens them when they try to nurse.

It is at this time that humans intervene and "socialize" the puppies. When a puppy is handled for short periods of time by humans, from the fifth week of puppyhood on, that animal grows to be highly adaptive to living with humans. However, it is extremely important that these short spans of affectionate handling be limited to once a day and that the dog remain with its litter for the rest of the time. This assures the puppy's socialization to both humans and dogs.

The Eighth Week to the Sixteenth Week (Final Phase of Socialization)

The puppy is now capable of vocalizing with greater variety and maturity. Although pups tend to cry less, when they are in strange places they will bark, which indicates an assertive attitude. Coordination is much improved and with it one sees the ability to run developing. Most of the social development that began in the fourth week becomes much more pronounced in the eighth, such as pack movement and antagonistic tendencies. Combative play becomes more intense as a means of developing the ranking order of dominance and subordination. This has a lasting effect, resulting in timid dogs, even-tempered dogs, or overly aggressive dogs.

For this reason, researchers have concluded that a dog experiencing human handling as a socializing technique should be removed from the litter and taken to its new home with a human family between the eighth and twelfth weeks. By removing the puppies at this time the last vestiges of weaning are automatically ended and the effects of a developing dominance order, detrimental to living with humans, are avoided. Assuming the puppy has been handled since the fourth week, it is now ready to make the transition to living as a pet and accepting some small amount of obedience training, including the beginning of housebreaking.

At this stage of the dog's life he has the capacity to become an engaging, well-trained companion, providing he is allowed to develop self-confidence as an individual dog with worth and value. This can be achieved by ensuring that the young dog is not isolated or left alone for long periods of time; by giving him a great deal of positive attention; and by short obedience training sessions that provide the opportunity for much-needed praise. At the end of the twelfth week, your dog enters his juvenile period, ready for complete obedience training and all the pleasures of being an adult dog.

Between eight and sixteen weeks, personality based on

dominance and subordination takes full shape. In a pack environment a young dog takes his permanent place in the social structure until circumstances dictate the necessity for change. The same is true if the young dog remains with his litter mates in a kennel.

Anytime after six months, a dog is physically capable of mating and renewing the cycle. When a human family takes a puppy into their home, this cycle is still ongoing, with the human environment substituting for the canine factors. Ideally, a pet dog should take a subordinate position in relation to his human family (or pack). This can come about only if the dog is adaptive to humans and if the humans in the family take the leadership position (without becoming overbearing). When the pet owner understands this, he or she is prepared for what comes naturally. In the beginning, all puppy behavior is based on instinct and the predilection toward pack structure.

Three to Five Months

This is one of the most delightful times to enjoy a puppy. At this age the dog is fully aware of himself and his environment. He wants to explore, examine, test, and get into everything in his new home. His desire to play is very great, as is his curiosity about you and his new family. You are the dog's environment. Everything that he will be is determined by how you behave toward him. This is the exact period when the closest ties are made and the deepest relationships between dogs and humans are developed. If you are sensitive, kind, soft-spoken, and loving, that is how your dog will be. However, never forget that *you* are the leader of his pack.

Medically speaking, this is the period to watch out for

teething pain and symptoms of internal parasites. If you have been living with the dog for more than a month, he should be housebroken or paper-trained by now. Basic obedience as a way of life is just around the corner, and the puppy should be partially trained, at the very least.

Five to Seven Months

You can no longer refer to your dog as a little puppy any more. He is now in his juvenile stage and fast moving toward adulthood unless he is one of the very large breeds. The giant dog breeds mature much later (usually by eighteen months) than the small breeds. Of course, many dogs of this age are still teething and experiencing the painful discomfort of losing their milk teeth and breaking through with permanent ones. There is a strong possibility that your dog is engaging in destructive chewing because of this.

Your dog should definitely be housebroken or paper-trained by this time. If he is not he has either been trained improperly or not at all. There is always a possibility that your dog has a medical problem. A dog infested with internal parasites such as common roundworms cannot control himself and will go off his house-training. See a veterinarian and have the dog examined. If your dog is healthy and continues to soil the house, you can seek professional help or refer to Chapter Five, "Getting Your Dog Under Control," or Chapter Seven, "Misbehavior."

This is a deceptive time for the novice dog owner living in the city and keeping an indoor dog. Here you have a dog that appears to be older than a puppy and almost fully grown. It is a mistake to treat a dog of this age as you would an adult. His body is still in a state of growth, perhaps its greatest stage of physical development. The dog's coat is not fully grown in yet, and he may not be fully protected from drafts, chills, and inclement weather. If it is winter, provide him with a warm sweater or coat for going outdoors. Dry the dog well if he gets wet. You may not have to be this cautious if your dog's coat is long and full. In some breeds, the fur is fully developed at an early age. This is true of Siberian Huskies, Alaskan Malamutes, Samoyeds, and similar breeds. If it is summer, keep the dog cool by *not* clipping his long-haired coat; it provides insulation from the heat.

The outdoor dog who usually resides in rural areas need not wear a winter sweater or be dried off when wet. If the dog is outdoors most of the time, even his puppy coat will suffice. Of course, you must judge how long a dog should stay outdoors on very cold days.

At this age, give serious consideration to grooming and personal hygiene. It will be helpful to consult a dog care or grooming book, or seek the services of a professional groomer. Dogs must be taught at an early age to tolerate the procedures of dog grooming, particularly being bathed, combed, brushed, and trimmed.

Seven to Twelve Months

These may be referred to as the frisky months because at no other time will your dog be as playful, as mischievous, as amusing, or as irritating as he is at this age.

3

THE DOG
THE PUPPY
WILL BECOME

There is no such thing as an ugly puppy. They are all appealing and lovable, and many of us want to take every one of them home on first sight. With their large, pleading eyes and impish stances, they creep right into your heart and make it very difficult to choose one from the other. Once you've made your selection, however, you are the proud owner of a *pup-in-a-poke* because, like most first-time dog owners, you have no idea what you are getting into or the kind of a dog your puppy will grow to be.

It is impossible for the inexperienced dog owner to predict with any certainty how an eight-to-twelve-week-old puppy is going to turn out. Not even the dog's pedigree (family tree) is a guarantee of what the dog will look like or how close he will come to the standard of perfection for his breed. However, with the exception of good health, your main concern should be your puppy's behavior and how it will develop. Because most breeders take pride in the quality of their dogs, they will try to steer you to a good one. Many people shopping for a dog are not interested in competing in dog shows and consequently will be offered an animal of "pet quality." Do not be put off by the term or upset because the breeder will not sell you a "show quality" dog. Breeders are interested in having those dogs "campaigned" for a champion title in the show ring. It's why they breed dogs.

"Pet quality" dogs are pure-bred dogs that for some minor reason will never be shown. They are almost always healthy dogs with sound temperaments and that is the most important consideration for someone shopping for a companion animal. A puppy of pet quality quite often has one slight flaw that makes the difference between a pet and a winner in the show ring. Perhaps one hind leg turns out just a bit or the nose color is slightly off or there may be some other "flaw" that would keep the dog from winning blue ribbons. Pet quality dogs are, for the most part, among the best companions in the world.

A Healthy Puppy

Behavioral problems become much more intense when a puppy is in bad health. In some cases, health problems create behavioral problems. That is just another good reason why you should try to select a puppy in a good state of health. The puppy's eyes should be smooth, shiny and unblemished. Its teeth should look clean and new, like white pins set firmly in bright pink gums. Running fluid or crusty discharge from the youngster's eyes, ears, or nose is a sign of illness. The condition of the coat is an important barometer of health. If the dog's hair coat is not healthy-looking with a low-luster and void of bare patches be suspicious. If there is one puppy that is obviously in bad health, either in the pet shop or in a breeder's kennel, do not pick any dog from that group. Pass them by.

Look for unnatural markings or discoloration in the eyes. A puppy with a distended belly may have internal parasites or some other ailment. Of course, if the dog has just been fed, the belly will be somewhat distended, which is *not* a sign of poor health. View the pups two hours after feeding time.

Do not pick a dog that is unusually fat, thin, or different from the rest of the litter in any radical way. Watch for continual rubbing of the eyes, ears, or nose. This could be a sign of skin disease, external parasites (mites), or infection. If a pup is continually scratching its body, it is a sign of fleas or a medical problem pertaining to the skin. Some puppies are born deaf. Test for deafness by gently clapping your hands behind the dog and watching for a response. If there is none, check further. Do not purchase a puppy that is suffering from diarrhea or bloody stools.

Find out if the puppy has been inoculated. Ask what it was inoculated for, when, and which type of inoculation was used. Make note of the information. It will be valuable when the dog is taken for its first regular visit to a veterinarian. Ask for a written guarantee that the puppy can be returned if, after a veterinary examination, he is found to be in poor health.

Do not leave without official papers from the American Kennel Club if the dog is represented as AKC registered. In most cases the litter has been registered and you will be given a form to mail to the AKC with the registration fee, in order to register the individual puppy. This is a proper procedure.

Temperament

One of the most important aspects of owning a dog is knowing what his temperament is and learning how to adjust your handling techniques to it, as well as learning what changes in the dog are possible. For example, it makes no sense handling a shy or timid dog in too strict or over-bearing a manner. And, heaven-forbid, hollering at or threatening these dogs only worsens their problems. Mishandling a shy dog will create behavioral problems additional to those you are already trying to solve. A shy dog that is threatened may eventually bite the person threatening him, or he may just hide under the bed indefinitely, quaking with fear and rage. A timid dog that is hollered at may urinate where he stands and piddle all over the house at the least likely times. Obviously, you must handle your dog in a manner that is appropriate for his temperament, in addition to the way you train him. But before you can do the right thing you must know something about canine temperament.

Dog temperament is one of those terms we think we understand until it comes time to define it. What exactly is dog temperament and does it have the same connotation as the term "temperamental"? When the prima donna stalks off the stage of an opera house because the tenor stepped in front of her during her aria, she is considered temperamental. When your dog bites the mailman on the seat of his pants, the dog is behaving according to his *temperament*. There is a difference between the two performances. The prima donna is indulging her ego, which may well be part of her personality, but is controllable and not typical of everybody. The dog, on the other hand, is doing what his genes, breeding, and upbringing have conditioned him to do.

It is difficult to determine when the word "temperament" was first used in relation to dogs, and in what sense. This may go back to Elizabethan literary references to dogs that were hostile and unflattering: "Take heed of yonder dog! Look, when he fawns, he bites"—*Richard III*.

Temperament, from the Latin *temperamentum*, means

"due measure or proportion," related to the medieval belief that the mix of certain *humors* in the body (an ancient term for body fluids) determined one's disposition or temperament. These fluids were blood (cheerful), lymph (lethargic), yellow bile (hot-tempered), and black bile (depressed). It is more accurate to refer to the various temperaments of dogs, rather than to dogs that are temperamental.

There are four elements that influence a dog's temperament: inherited genes, breed characteristics, imposed environmental influences, and learning as a result of experience or teaching. The genetic factor is usually the most powerful consideration. When a dog's parents and grandparents are of a specific physical, mental, and emotional quality, chances are great that many of the puppies will be similar. If a dog is a good example of its breed, it will possess much of that breed's predictable temperamental characteristics. For example, German Shepherd Dogs are expected to be protective and highly territorial, while most terriers are decision-makers (about hunting and guarding matters) and difficult to persuade once they have made up their minds about something. It is profitable for the new dog owner to learn as much as possible about the characteristics of a dog's breed from canine reference books and informed dog people.

Among the environmental influences on temperament there is the matter of socialization during the critical period of a puppy's first weeks of life, in addition to how it is treated and handled by humans and animals in the latter stages of puppyhood and adolescence. Unless you purchased your dog from a good breeder you can only guess what happened before you got him.

Learning as an influence on temperament is a more elusive matter. It depends upon the circumstances of the learning experiences, or who is teaching what and to what degree it is being taught. On the negative side, a puppy that has been hit severely may become a ferociously aggressive or a painfully frightened, shy dog. On the positive side, a puppy that is treated lovingly and given humane obedience training may learn to be a dog with a basic temperament, which is to say, gentle, devoted, and obedient.

But if you know something about the various temperament categories, it is not difficult to determine what your dog is like and how to handle him. Temperaments can be divided into at least six separate categories, plus variations and combinations of the six. The six primary temperaments are: shy, aggressive, nervous, stubborn, sedate, and basic.

Shy/Timid Temperament

Admit it. The most appealing puppy in the new litter is the adorable one that hides in the corner, almost blushing with hesitation while the others run to yap and lick your finger. Most often the shy baby is the dog that gets selected over the others, and most often it is the shy dog that becomes a domestic disaster.

Shyness in humans indicates a quality of personal insecurity and an inability to meet new people and situations in the most direct manner. Shy people need more time than other types to face the realities of change. They are extremely cautious, somewhat withdrawn, easily embarrassed, awkward in the presence of others and, most important, lacking in self-confidence. These qualities also apply to shy dogs.

The shy dog can almost always be found hiding under a table, a chair, or a bed. He doesn't greet people when they come into the house. Shy dogs are afraid of noises and run away when they are petted. They jump with fear if something is accidentally dropped. When you put a leash on the dog, his ears go down and he cowers with a drooping head. Some shy dogs are well-adjusted with their owners, but will hide when a stranger appears.

When Fido runs to hide under a table as a friend enters the house, it is laughingly shrugged off as shyness. Everyone agrees he is just a Muppet Baby. Case closed. That is a big mistake. Those two eyes peering out from under the dining room table may be watching for imagined enemies to approach and then attack. When an animal is frightened enough, it may become aggressive and surprise everyone. Your little dog may change from a shy dog to an aggressive dog in an instant and bite your neighbor on the ankle as he turns to leave the room. Uninitiated dog owners tend to think of canine shyness as something cute and lovable. It is not. In reality, the shy dog needs help and special consideration before someone gets hurt, including the dog.

There are several reasons for canine shyness. The first is genetic. Behavior, like everything else, is greatly influenced by those vague, hard to understand gene pools. The whole point of developing pure-bred animals and charting their family trees through pedigrees is to influence and predict a puppy's physical and mental potential. Understanding a pedigree can give a prospective dog owner a fair, if hardly foolproof, idea of what to expect. Ask an experienced dog breeder about interpreting a pedigree, or write to the American Kennel Club (51 Madison Avenue, NY, NY 10010). A pedigree is a dog's family tree and indicates quite clearly who his parents, grandparents, great-grandparents, etc. were. It also indicates if there were any Champions of Record in his line. It can be a valuable reference tool for a knowledgeable dog person.

Some dogs become shy if they remain with their litter past twelve weeks of age. From twelve to fifteen weeks, puppies begin to develop a dominant-subordinate pattern and establish their positions in the litter, which by now can be considered a dog pack. It is likely that when your shy dog was a very young puppy he was not as strong or as assertive as his litter-mates, and was denied a teat or a warm, comfortable position next to his mother. Such pups are often bullied by the others and constantly forced into a subordinate position within the litter. If this was done with severity, your pet will have grown into a shy dog.

And then there are those dogs who were not shy when they were born, never exposed to the rigors of pack existence at an early age but, rather, were made shy by human behavior (or misbehavior). A frightened puppy entering a new home can be turned into a shy dog by overpowering authority, or physical or mental abuse. Isolation can create a shy (or aggressive) dog. A firecracker, auto backfire, or gunshot can alter a puppy's personality, as can constant smacks on the snout for every infraction of household rules. Overexuberant children, domineering adults, and highly demanding dog owners in general can all create the negative quality of shyness in the best of dogs. Even overpowering body language from well-intended humans can create a shy dog. Fear, terror, and punishment are occasionally the cause, also. Outmoded, inhumane housebreaking techniques are the greatest cause of all. These include hitting the dog, hollering at him, and employing humiliating punishments, such as rubbing his nose in his own mess.

An important way to avoid the problem of shyness is to acquire a dog that is not born with it. You can achieve this by avoiding puppies past sixteen weeks of age if they are still living with their litters and behaving in a shy manner.

Do not pick an insecure dog that is timid and retiring, no matter how it tugs at your heartstrings. A normal puppy should be curious and somewhat assertive. If it has been properly introduced to human handling at an early age (socialized), it will not be frightened of strangers. This is important. A shy *puppy* can be endearing. A shy *dog* can be dangerous and difficult to live with. It is likely to bite someone sooner or later, at the slightest provocation, if it is frightened enough.

If you are already living with a shy dog, you must handle him with loving care. Be patient in all matters, but especially when the dog cowers or runs from a situation that frightens him. Make few demands on the animal and virtually envelop him with affection. Talk to the dog in soft, soothing tones and apply leash discipline in only the gentlest way. Do not punish your dog. Behavior problems must be dealt with through teaching and correction. Through intimate contact such as reassuring petting sessions you may, at the least, allow the dog to be confident with you. Do not allow anyone to deal with the animal in a harsh or aggressive manner. A shy dog can be just as lovable as any other. We all have parental instincts and must allow them to come to the surface for a frightened friend.

Aggressive Temperament

Some people never get to enjoy their dogs because their home companions are aggressive or even dangerous. Complicating their lives may be confrontations, threats, law suits, and lost relationships with friends, relatives, and neighbors. Utility workers refuse to enter their property. Letter carriers avoid them. Delivery men won't deliver. Telephone repairmen leave them on hold. These are the results of dogs that bite, bark, chase, threaten, bully, growl, and rush or sneak up on tradesmen, neighbors, friends, and relatives.

An aggressive dog could merely be unfriendly and intimidating with its sharp stare and rigid body language, or one that threatens people or other dogs with barks and rushing movements. Canine aggressiveness is meant to dominate members of the family, including children and other pets. It is how wild dogs or wolves become the leader of the pack. The alpha wolf (or leader) must fight aggressively to gain his position, and then behave with aggressive assertion and belligerence toward the lesser pack members in order to maintain it.

Some aggressive dogs bully people and other dogs by running at them and then stopping, by blocking a person's path with the length of their bodies, by pushing or slamming with shoulders or hips, or by using all available means of intimidation to get their way. Dominance is the name of the game. Unfortunately, it sometimes gets rougher than that.

An aggressive dog that is asserting his dominance is often one that does not hold back his aggression. He may attack anyone or anything that violates his territory. It is dominance with a vengeance.

A dog may also be aggressive because he is frightened of being attacked by those who enter his territory as a stranger. Aggressive warning behavior involves various forms of body language, such as direct stares, raised hackles, raised ears, snarling mouth showing teeth, arched body, and a tail that is pointing upward or downward in a straight vertical line. The bite may range from a warning snap to a nip to a full bite as he shakes his head from side to side, which is meant to do as much damage as possible. In addition, such a dog may chase, spring, pounce, or jump upon his target.

Aggressive dogs are either *dominant-aggressive* or *fear-aggressive* (or combinations of the two). The behavior of a dominant-aggressive dog is much more dangerous and is based on his desire to boss and bully all those around him. Fear-aggressive behavior is less dangerous, but frightening; it stems from the dog's anxiety about someone or something. Interestingly, most dog bites come from fear-aggressive dogs.

Within every breed there are individual dogs that are more aggressive than the rest. Usually, they have inherited aggressive behavioral qualities from one or more of their parents or grandparents. Some dogs, however, are made aggressive by their experiences in the world. Abusive behavior will most certainly create an aggressive dog.

It is essential for those who live with dogs to understand the conditions that create the problems of aggressiveness. Sometimes it is not too late to alter the dog's lifestyle or conditioning.

Aggressive behavior is most often inherited. The genetic factor cannot be ignored. Dogs that have had little or no socialization may never adapt to living in a human environment and may become aggressive in time. Environmental experiences can also create aggressive behavior. This behavior is often formed by owners who mistakenly believe that they are teaching their dogs something by hitting them. Other causes are: lack of friendly relations, isolation, teasing, aggressive-type games (tug-of-war, mock fighting, etc.), or encouragement of protective behavior (from non-professionals).

A barking dog never bites? Don't you believe it. A barker's potential danger can be gauged by the ferocity of the barking and accompanying aggressive behavior. Like humans, many dogs have been genetically endowed with more aggressiveness than is good for them. A dog who growls and snarls at you from deep within his throat; chases people, bicycles or cars; snaps, nips and bullies is a potential biter. Many dogs snarl if anyone goes near their food or possessions, including their owners. All of these should be considered as unacceptable behaviors and not tolerated.

Dog owners should observe and try to understand their pets' idiosyncrasies and learn how to spot early warning signs of aggressive and fear behavior—and then act quickly before the dog actually bites someone. A growl is a dog's warning that he will bite you if you continue to do whatever you are doing. His rigid body language and direct stare into your eyes are the signs. Be careful.

Preventing aggressive behavior is the best hope for dogs and their owners. This has largely to do with the initial selection of a dog. If you select a puppy that does not bully the rest of the litter, does not frighten them away from the food bowl with snarls and growls, does not curl its lips, and allows a human to cradle it on its back, it does not have an aggressive temperament. A puppy that is not encouraged to bark or bite by a human with the misguided notion of creating a protection dog will probably grow into a happy, pleasant animal.

There are those who believe that having a dog who bites on their premises is a good security measure, like the presence of an attack or guard dog. But attack and guard dogs, such as those trained for the military, police, and industrial security firms, are not simply animals taught to bite. They are professionally trained working dogs and are absolutely obedient to their handlers. They do only what they are ordered to do and nothing more. Training your own "guard dog" is like placing a loose cannon on your property. A dog "trained" by an amateur for protection is not a guard dog at all, but merely a dog brought to a vicious state whose behavior is uncontrolled, unpredictable, and dangerous to everyone.

Dogs that bite do so primarily to defend their territory, possessions, or position of dominance. Some breeds (and some individual dogs) defend their homes with greater vigor than others and consider their human family as much their personal property as their food bowls. But, as any mailman can attest, dogs cannot always understand the difference between intruders and innocent strangers on lawful business. An innocent stranger can also be a child chasing a ball.

A dog who bites is not an asset and must be dealt with as soon as possible in tough, uncompromising terms. It is difficult and often impossible to solve serious biting behavior in dogs past ten months of age. If you own such a dog it is imperative to have him evaluated by a professional dog trainer or animal behaviorist, or both. Preventive action and some corrective techniques used on dogs younger than ten months of age significantly reduces all aggression problems. Be skeptical of any dog trainer or professional that "guarantees" a cure for aggressive behavior.

Nervous Temperament

A dog with a nervous temperament may be one with simply too much energy or present variations on the shy temperament. This is probably the most troublesome of all the temperaments for pet owners. The problems of nervous dogs are difficult to solve. Fear and anxiety in various degrees are the principal forces within this type of animal. A nervous dog cannot relax except when asleep, and then will prove to be a light sleeper. This dog will overreact to the slightest stimulus. When the owner returns home, even after just fifteen minutes, the dog will jump with uncontrolled excitement and wet the floor. He will wet the floor if he is scolded or given affection. It does not seem to matter. A nervous dog is often a chewer and will cause thousands of dollars worth of damage to the home when left alone or not closely supervised.

Some nervous dogs are afraid of traffic, afraid of going outdoors, afraid of strangers, and afraid of other dogs. Others are just the opposite. They are too exuberant and overactive in just about all situations. These high-strung pets are very often the result of poor commercial breeding. But there are environmental situations that can also cause this behavior. For example, if a dog has had several owners and was commanded in different ways each time, he may have developed a confusion leading to insecurity and an inability to please the current master. Leaving the old home represents a loss of territory and the familiar pack, which could result in nervousness. Some nervous dogs have simply acquired the inconsistent tendencies of their owners, reflecting nervous or neurotic behavior. A lack of social experience with the outer world can also create a frightened, anxiety-ridden dog, as can an auto backfire or gunshot at an impressionable age. Naturally, any physical or emotional abuse can destroy a perfectly normal dog and create a nervous wreck.

Nervous dogs pace back and forth and create nervous humans. They will follow their owners from room to room in a manner that indicates insecurity, rather than playfulness. This would indicate an animal that is afraid to be without its dominant figure or pack leader. The nervousness may be manifested by whining, barking excessively, sudden bursts of energy, heavy breathing, glassy gaze, and total dependence. Living with a nervous dog is a test of one's patience and love.

Some nervous dogs develop a canine version of nervousness from their human families who teach this behavior through interaction with the animal and by the example they set. When a dog becomes a substitute for another human being, chances are great that he will take on the characteristics of the human or humans around him, whatever they happen to be. Where there is a nervous dog, there may be a nervous person.

When isolating a dog's nervous characteristics from the many, many positive traits, the problems often seem worse than they really are and appear insurmountable. This is definitely not true. A nervous dog is eminently trainable. He requires more patience from his owner than usual. He needs more understanding and kindness than most dogs. The nervous dog should be handled by one member of the family in a quiet, gentle, and subdued manner. A dog of this temperament can also be a good and loving pet. He simply has problems that must be dealt with before they cause other more serious problems.

Stubborn Temperament

This quality may take many different forms, some of which are surprising. Within the same negative characteristics are passive resistance, obstinacy, and dug-in stubbornness. Some stubborn dogs actually throw temper tantrums. These may range from barking to running in circles to destructive chewing when left alone, although chewing may also be caused by other problems such as boredom, teething, and illness.

Some stubborn dogs will not walk ahead on their leashes when they do not wish to cooperate. They may go so far as refusing to walk at all. They are unwilling to obey commands or respond to corrections. When they are unwilling to cooperate, they may growl in a menacing tone or talk back by barking or yipping after being reprimanded. The most stubborn dogs will dig their heels into the ground and refuse to respond in the face of punishment, threats, pleading or bribery. They are not a barrel of laughs.

A stubborn dog is unwilling to obey your commands or respond to your corrections. He will sometimes growl in a menacing tone when his owner attempts to discipline him. It is a serious problem to have a dog with a stubborn temperament who also misbehaves. For instance, a stubborn dog who jumps on people is very difficult to stop. When you place the leash on him, he may fight it with his paws or his teeth and even growl at it. A stubborn dog can be very responsive but it takes harder work. Corrections, especially leash corrections, must be firm, along with a very firm tone of voice. Stubborn dogs must be convinced that you mean business. The stubborn dog must be made to realize that you mean it when a command is given and that he must obey it. Dogs of this temperament constantly fight the training process. It sometimes becomes a battle of wills with the outcome in serious question. It is absolutely necessary for the human member of the pack to be dominant, and gain control over the dog.

Dogs with stubborn temperaments require obedience training more than all others if they are going to live successfully in a human environment. Training can be successful if the trainer uses the teaching techniques of constant repetition of commands, firm corrections, dominant body language, an authoritative tone of voice, and taking an unyielding position of dominance.

Sedate Temperament

Dogs of this temperament are mostly the larger breeds such as Great Danes, Great Pyrenees, Newfoundlands, Mastiffs and Saint Bernards. Several of the medium-to-small breeds also tend to be sedate, and strains of them will contribute to this temperament in certain mixed-breeds. The Basset Hound and English Setter are among these types.

Although quite lovable, these are somewhat sensitive dogs that do not respond well to harsh tones or fast-paced demands. Sedate dogs are slow to the point of lethargy. They are lovable but not as demonstrative as other breeds or types. Dogs of this temperament sleep much of the time. Sedate dogs are responsive but in a very quiet, slow way. They do not have many of the normal problems associated with puppies. They don't jump very much. They don't nip. They don't chew. They're not excessive barkers.

When taking them out for walks, they tend to lag behind and may give the false impression that they are resisting your commands. The truth is they are simply slow walkers. They seem to think about everything before taking an action. Slowness must not be mistaken for stubbornness or lack of intelligence. With patience and proper training a sedate dog can be just as willing to please as any other.

Basic Temperament

This probably best describes the majority of domestic dogs, purebred, mixed-breed, or mongrel. These are the ones that are the easiest to train, the most willing to please, easygoing, sweet-natured, patient, and forbearing: they are the *basic dog*. These qualities cut across all breeds (including mongrels), all sizes, colors, and shapes. It is the true and natural disposition of the domestic dog, and is what makes him the wonderful companion animal that he is.

Dogs of the basic temperament are the easiest to train. They offer the least amount of difficulty and do not require special handling. The basic dog is curious and enthusiastic about learning anything you are willing to teach him. He can be trained with minimal effort and will respond to teaching techniques at a good rate of learning. Average corrections and ample praise work well for dogs of this temperament.

It is important to understand that the negative characteristics, as summarized in some of the temperament descriptions, are not necessarily negative to everyone. A shy dog or an aggressive dog may be exactly what some person may want or need. However, it is safe to say that if these characteristics are difficult to live with, they may be eliminated or certainly modified with the help of a solid obedience-training course. Simple dog obedience training solves most problem behavior in dogs. One may do-it-yourself, attend classes (contact your local animal shelter or humane society), or hire a professional for one-on-one dog training. These are the options available.

Home Life

Behavioral patterns in dogs develop early. Five-week-old puppies tend to imitate those that are around them the most—other dogs, who may be their parents and litter mates. It is the beginning of learned behavior, as opposed to behavior that develops instinctively. What happens to a dog in a new home the first weeks has a profound influence on his behavior for the rest of his life. Puppies tend to imitate the attitudes and emotional and physical actions of their human families. The way a human relates to his or her dog during the first few weeks that they're together helps determine the dog's behavioral patterns and plays a role in shaping the animal's temperament.

Before housebreaking or training of any kind it is important to *bond* with your new dog. What is meant by that is establishing a meaningful relationship with the dog. Human contact and expressions of welcome and affection make it easy for the young dog to establish himself as part of the family. This connects with his instinct to fit in by pleasing those in the family of higher rank in the social structure. Bonding involves the development of strong emotional ties and is seen in human relationships of every type.

A demanding, overpowering manner, introducing adult-style dog training, and expecting too much, too soon from a puppy can obstruct or even prevent the bonding process. The potential for a loving, joyful relationship may wane under such conditions and with it the possibility of many years of pleasurable companionship.

A recent myth of dog ownership is: *Never spoil your puppy*. This is simply not correct. It is a popular misconception that you must constantly discipline a puppy and never let him get away with things. Expect puppies to do most things wrong in the beginning. It is our responsibility to educate ourselves so that the appropriate methods are used to teach as we nurture a little dog.

For most dogs maturity is achieved at the end of the first year of life. (Giant breeds mature later.) Typically, puppies are taken to their new homes between two and three months of age. Try to compare a three-to-five-month-old puppy with a kindergarten child; a five-to-seven-month-old dog with a juvenile; and a seven-to-twelve-month-old dog with a teenager.

How much would you expect from a child in nursery school or even kindergarten? How much can you expect? It almost answers itself. Do not misunderstand. This is an important time for puppies as well as children. Rules must be established, but they are more like boundary posts in the beginning. Puppies must negotiate a learning process before we can expect them to behave like obedient angels. The learning process must not be harsh or unforgiving. A firm, demanding approach to training comes later, usually in the sixth month, depending on the nature of the dog.

The Impact of Housebreaking on Temperament

More mistakes are made by humans during housebreaking than at any other time. Many novice dog owners are simply not used to dealing with the body's waste matter and become quite upset at the sight. Consequently, physical punishments and hysterical yelling become misconstrued as training techniques and lead to serious negative effects on the dog's temperament. Severe scolding, harsh finger-pointing, hitting, and hollering will damage the bond, and create insecurity and bewilderment, in addition to hampering positive learning in a young dog. They can also result in shyness, aggressiveness, nervousness, and even stubbornness.

Housebreaking a dog involves various techniques that condition him away from his natural inclinations. One should never forget that housebreaking is a set of behaviors meant to please humans and is essentially artificial and unnatural for dogs. Be kind, patient, and understanding.

No matter what technique is used—crate or confinement to a kitchen, with or without newspapers—when a puppy makes a mistake, do not be abusive. Hollering accomplishes nothing, and striking a puppy (or rubbing his nose in his own mess) is inhumane, ineffective, and destructive to his personality. *Correct him only if you catch him in the act.* Corrections (not punishments) should involve nothing more than a simple "NO!" and a speedy removal to his toilet place. (Please refer to Chapter Six, "House Training Your Dog.")

You will achieve much better results when housebreaking a puppy by establishing the place where it is acceptable for him to relieve himself; by creating a feeding-watering-walking schedule and adhering to it; by eliminating the odor of past "mistakes"; and by confining the little dog to one small area when no one can watch for the signs that he has to go out.

Obedience Training and Its Effect on Temperament

Few consider that obedience training can have a very significant influence on temperament. If human temperament or the behavior that stems from it can be modified, so can dog behavior be influenced. Dog obedience training is the key to acceptable dog behavior. Dog training is nothing more than behavior modification brought about by creating new conditioned reflexes in the dog and by manipulating the dog's natural pack and social inclinations. (Please refer to Chapter Five, "Getting Your Dog Under Control.")

Patience and understanding help the process. A puppy should not be treated with the same firmness as a fully grown dog and requires more time to learn. Training can begin as early as eight weeks old, but must be tailored to the dog's age, temperament, and learning pace.

Do not forget that your primary concern during the first months with your dog is to create a bond between him and the family. Control your temper (even when the puppy frustrates you). Learn to control your voice so that you are gently demanding and not harsh, coaxing instead of dictatorial, happy sounding rather than hysterical. Bear in mind that you must first teach a dog what you want before you can expect him to do it. And "correct" him rather than punish him for not obeying your commands. Consider the possibility that there may be something lacking in your teaching efforts. Hire a professional dog trainer or obtain a good dog training book, and use it.

Before attempting to solve your dog's behavior problems or begin any type of training, you should try to determine his temperament type. This will definitely help you achieve the best results possible and at the same time help create a more meaningful relationship between your dog and his family. Your ability to communicate with your dog enhances everything from family life to training your dog. Whether to go easy or be firm depends on how well you understand your dog's temperament. Although six temperament categories are referred to in this chapter, it is obvious that all dogs do not fall neatly into these classifications. It is correct to say that the temperaments of all dogs are made up of combinations of these classifications. You might have a dog that is nervous-aggressive or shy-sedate, etc. If that best describes your dog, then decide which quality is the dominant one and alter your manner to that one.

If you can accept the proposition that pets do not serve as substitute people but rather offer a unique relationship independent of all others, then you can accept the idea that they possess their own personalities. Pets belong to themselves as individuals, and their temperaments, although alterable to some degree, exist as part of who they are. To learn more about your dog's temperament is to discover why you love him.

4

A DOG
IN THE FAMILY

Like dogs, we are highly social creatures and do our best when we live our lives with others. Of course, our definition of *family* has changed drastically. We no longer think exclusively of mother, father, and children when we try to characterize a family. A family can be a mother and a daughter; a nephew and an aunt; two friends; two lovers; or one person and a dog. We now accept the idea that a family is simply two or more creatures sharing their lives. A dog's need for family life is at least as great as a human's need and probably even greater. Don't forget, a dog is a pack animal and "pack" is just another word for family.

Every instinctive behavior that dogs are born with has something to do with their need to function well within their family (or pack). The point is, your best opportunity for living a relatively problem-free existence with your dog is to provide him with a reasonable family life. That involves understanding how a dog fits into the human environment as a member of the family. Whatever exists within and around your family makes up that environment. For better or for worse, the dog you have taken in, like the child you have borne, the spouse to whom you have committed, or the friend with whom you live, is a part of your life now. He may add or subtract, strengthen or weaken your day-to-day existence. You cannot ignore the fact. No matter what your reason for getting a dog, his impact on every member of the family is great. The dog's need for friendship, love, and care are a shared responsibility, and impact greatly on the dog.

Dogs and Adults

Probably the single most important thing for adults to understand about living with a dog is his need to have a leader of the pack. This is not an easy thing for many new dog owners and it creates many behavioral problems as a result.

The inability to be assertive with pets is usually based on a fear that the animal will no longer love the dog owner if corrected, or disciplined, or even commanded in a firm manner. (This same misguided kindness is often seen in parents of misbehaved children.) Complicating matters further is the notion that it is cruel to force a pet to stop doing something, even if it is doing something annoying or destructive.

An important fact of life is to understand that no dog will stop loving you once you decide to take control of his behavior. In fact, it will strengthen your rapport with your pet. Asserting yourself with a pet is not an act of cruelty. It isn't even a violation of your animal's true nature. Do not get entangled in the "Born Free" syndrome where everything you do to and for your dog is taken as a violation of the animal's natural inclinations. That attitude has hurt more animals than helped them. For example, think of what can happen to unleashed dogs in city traffic or dogs that are allowed to bark, or even bite, without being corrected.

Adult Attitudes

Biting your dog's face or kissing his tail has more to do
with emotional extremities than physical ones. An adult's
behavior toward dogs has much to do with attitudes toward
animals that he or she has developed over the years. These
attitudes are a key factor in shaping the dog/human relationship. Whether you totally dominate your dog or allow
yourself to be treated as his pet is greatly influenced by how
you feel about all animals and yourself. A dog that runs the
show is going to be a sort of canine mother-in-law, insisting
on having her way, working you over with intimidation,
guilt, and other manipulations. The reverse of that situation
is the dog that cringes in fear whenever you enter the room
because he's not sure whether you're going to yell, hit, or
just scowl. In either situation, both dog and human are act-
ing upon each other in less than satisfactory terms. Maybe
your dog is not crazy—maybe he just behaves that way
because of his home life. There are alternative lifestyles.

Setting aside the genetic influences and the early socialization factor, your dog's behavior is going to reflect the
lifestyle he lives with his family. If a dog lives in a neurotic
situation, you can rely on his being neurotic. For example,
many people use food for neurotic reasons that go beyond
the need to satisfy their own hunger. If that type of person
keeps a dog, chances are good that the dog is going to
become portly and relate to food in the same neurotic
manner as those around him. This is also greatly influenced
by whether that adult views animals as closely related to
humans or not. Here, again, we return to human attitudes
toward animals. There can be no doubt that attitudes about
animals and psychological distortion play an important role

in shaping pet-owner behavior which, in turn, affects a pet dog's behavior. Dog training can make a significant difference in making a dog manageable. However, it will not necessarily alter the distorted behavior of a dog if the humans do not alter their behavior toward the dog.

Have you ever witnessed a dachshund having a psychosomatic asthma attack? The poor dog hacks and wheezes and honks in situations where he cannot have his own way. Fat dogs that eat until their eyes cross overeat just for the attention. Many dogs deliberately disobey commands and rules of conduct in order to get attention. This form of distorted behavior in dogs is usually the result of human indulgence and an inappropriate attitude about dogs which creates the reticence to just say "NO."

Dogs develop the canine version of their owners' attitudes and behavior through interaction with the family and by the example they set. Competing for attention, imagined illnesses, and the entire range of distorted human behavior in dogs is often learned from the dog's human caretakers and, indeed, becomes an integral part of the relationship. Still, if a dog is young, he can be retrained away from abnormal behavior, providing there is no physical or genetic deficiency. Have the dog examined by a veterinarian to be certain he is in good health. Hire a professional dog trainer and get the animal under control. Engage in some degree of self-examination to see if there is any opportunity for change in relation to the dog. Whenever a dog is behaving inappropriately for a dog, ask yourself the question: "Is there anything in my attitude that contributes to this dog's unacceptable behavior?" Human attitudes toward animals are not difficult to change once you understand how they can be harmful to achieving a successful relationship with your dog.

No matter why you start out wanting a dog, it is always possible to reevaluate and change your reasons. And for those who have never thought about it, here is an opportunity to develop a point of view that may present your own dogs to you in new and more meaningful terms.

No matter how domesticated dogs are, and even though they almost never experience the lust for freedom that their wild cousins enjoy, they are, nevertheless, an important aspect of nature. Dogs connect us with the unpaved world of the plains, forests, deserts, mountains, and jungles. Stroking the nape of a Labrador Retriever can conjure a feeling of rushing water and roasted fowl on a crackling spit. The bloodhound's cry from a distant woods and the aggressive Basenji on a jungle hunt are there for the imagining. The darting lope of a gazehound racing on the sands of the Sinai can easily transport the homebound dog owner to anyplace in the imagination. The German Shepherd Dog and his fellow worker, the Collie, bring to skyscraper apartments the smell of grass and the image of sheep grazing in a pasture. The dogs have all been there at one time or another and keep us in touch with nature because of their uninhibited ways.

In our artificial surroundings dogs remind us that we are part of nature and also live off the land. Keeping a dog is a civilized and convenient way to live with some small portion of the natural life we have given up so long ago. For this reason, and for the simple pleasure of friendship, it is worth developing a new attitude toward dogs.

Assertiveness Training for Dog Owners

Dogs who poke their noses into the garbage can, jump on you, or have other annoying habits must be handled in a special way. They require strong leadership and domination. The basis of assertiveness training for pet owners is the knowledge that their pet's very life depends on humans being dominant and animals being subordinate.

In the wild, dogs (or wolves) develop a highly structured social hierarchy based on dominance and subordination. The dominant *canid* or leader of the pack makes all decisions about mating, hunting, territory and fighting. The pack leader is always the biggest, strongest, and most intelligent, commanding respect from all other members of the pack.

In the dog/human equation, think of the family as the pack and all the humans as the leaders. *The family dog must be considered subordinate to all the human family members*. This doesn't require an overbearing or abusive manner. Hollering or hitting the animal isn't the answer. Instead, your assertiveness should be expressed by how you speak and move, and how persistent and demanding you become. Your attitude should convey to the dog that things must be done your way, not his. It must be an internal quality or aspect of your personality. If you do not feel like a pack leader, then pretend to be one. Think of yourself as an actor and play the role.

Behave like someone who holds the leash rather than someone clipped to it. Remember that you are the provider of food, water, shelter, love, indeed, life itself, and then act accordingly. If it weren't for you, your dog might not have a home. It's not necessary to assume the role of commanding officer of an infantry brigade in order to assert yourself. The firm-but-gentle manner of a concerned parent will achieve the best results. Dogs, like children, feel better knowing that someone is in charge and that things are under control.

This may be difficult with some dogs, especially those devilishly clever terriers, Dachshunds, Cocker Spaniels, and other breeds that know how to get their own way with humans. But never let it be said that you were outsmarted by your dog. The next time he attempts to steal food from the table or whines at the door when you are not ready for a walk, think about what you are doing and why you are doing it and then assert yourself. One of the best ways to do this is by exclaiming "NO," in a loud, firm tone of voice.

"NO" is an authoritative, corrective tool and should be used for negative behavior only. That is essential. "NO" should be a firm reprimand that comes from the diaphragm, a muscle separating your stomach from your chest. Take in a deep breath and allow your stomach to expand with air. Say the word "NO" as you release the air. Not even the most stubborn, aggressive dog will doubt you. Once you've established that your "NO" really means no, be consistent about it. Never back down.

Dogs and Children

Childhood, at its best, is a half-forgotten dream. Parents remember the laughter and the crying, clothes gone small, and the incredible responsibility for their children's health, character, education, and happiness. In these pursuits, the presence of a dog is of fabulous value. Getting a dog for a kid is like getting a teacher, a therapist, a parent, and a playmate all rolled into one lovable scamp, full of mischief and goodness. No matter how useful dogs are in our society as sentries, guide dogs, hearing-ear dogs, and all the rest, the large majority of them are acquired for the benefit of children; for their pleasure, to be sure, but more for their development. And there is no finer companion for most dogs than a kind, happy child. They are good for each other. Dogs enjoy playing follow-the-leader or being the leader. With a kid they get to do both, sooner or later. A kid and a dog make each other happy, and that's a fact of life.

Of all that children derive from their pets, including understanding birth, death, growth, and relationships, the most worthwhile lesson is leadership. Leadership is not meant here in the sense of Victorian platitudes or militaristic virtues, but rather in the vital areas of independence, self-sufficiency and competent self-management. If leadership is understood as the willingness to assume responsibility, to make decisions, and to risk failure, then a child taking care of a pet is, indeed, involved with leadership. Although all dogs should be subordinate to all humans, including children, they do tend to assume a role of responsibility for kids, in many situations.

Most parents feel that pet dogs have much to teach children. Of course, they are right. What professionals are finally coming to accept, parents have always known instinctively: that pets give children an opportunity to learn about life. Even when a pet is hurt, or dies, or is lost, it teaches the child what it is like to be human. It is not a negative experience if parents help the child to live through his or her grief and mourning over the death of a pet, if they do not try to hide or repress it but rather share it with them. It is worth crying about. It is how we learn about pain. When these things happen to humans, they are better understood by children who have lived with pets.

Pals or Siblings

Dogs and kids are as natural together as ice cream on a stick. Long before the creation of Chicken McNuggets and the Nintendo game, kids and their pets have been enjoying the better part of childhood together. It should come as no surprise. Remember, Mickey Mouse's pet was Pluto (a dog).

Pets are good friends but also members of the family. Acquiring a pet may be the only opportunity a child will ever have to choose a relative. The pet connection could easily become the most valuable experience your child will have, short of school and four years with an orthodontist. That is why it is a good thing for parents to allow their kids the wonderful experience of involvement with a dog.

Dogs and children enjoying each other only seems like magic. One might take a purely clinical view and suggest that, because of a child's limited experience and young intelligence, he or she and the dog share a mutual perception of the world. Or, one might say that children and young dogs are in a constant state of learning, which is evident in the way they play. Another idea has to do with pack behavior on the part of the dog and socializing behavior on the part of the child. Both are trying to establish their positions in society as well as reinforce those positions. While the child attempts to understand his or her environment, the dog instinctively accepts it. This may be the main difference between the two. Luckily, the child's curiosity and the dog's understanding of nature fit hand-in-glove and form a profitable partnership.

The bond that forms between a dog and a child is a firm link that is difficult to break. Child/dog relationships are extremely durable. A kid pulls his dog's tail and the dog knocks the kid down and steps on his face. They may both end up in tears, but that is really between the two of them and by no means indicates that they should be permanently separated. They will work it out quickly. Nothing short of violence can come between a child and a dog. They seek each other out and quickly become good friends as long as circumstances will allow. It is in the understanding of this bond between children and their dogs that parents can help shape a successful relationship between the two. In doing so they will be giving their children and their dog the gift of each other.

But sometimes there is trouble in paradise. A dog, like the arrival of a new child, can inadvertently become a source of friction. Most brothers and sisters compete with one another for parental attention and favor. The competition can be comical, serious, or totally absurd in its forms and directions. Absolute equality and parity are demanded of harassed and hassled parents by the bickering siblings. The combination of one dog and several kids has the makings of a potential nightmare for a mother and father who have had it up to here.

It would be wise always to walk the dog out of the competitive storm at the first sign of arguments concerning the dog. At this point, it is best for the dog not to be the focus of the children's anger. It is not really good for the children or the dog. Without getting involved in their argument, you can inform them that they are upsetting the dog (not to mention their bedraggled parents). Although the problems between siblings vary, this one has something to do with the ability to share. The children must be told that the dog is to be shared by the entire family and they must not tear the animal apart. Schedules, appointments, and the ability to take turns with the dog are essential. They might even be convinced to play with the dog together.

Sometimes, unwitting parents find themselves the rival of the dog for the children's attention or, more serious, the children competing with the dog for a parent's attention.

These are situations that are easy to adjust but must be taken care of before the problem becomes serious. If the dog seems to favor one child over another, it is inevitable that jealousy will be the result. But remember, dogs will accept whatever attention you decide you can give them. They start out neutral and can be brought back to neutral from any imbalance that grows. If the dog figures into any feelings of jealousy between the kids, it is time to sort it all out by having a family talk and clearing the air. Just keep pointing out that the dog belongs to himself and is to be enjoyed by everyone in the family. He is a living creature and not an object or possession. The dog has rights, too.

Choosing a Dog

Dogs are dynamic playmates for children, particularly once they are past the age of six. Most dogs love kids and in many cases feel responsible for their well-being and safety. In turn, kids who take care of dogs are able to apply what they've learned about kindness and responsibility to caring for people.

The final selection of a pet must be a parental decision. If you let the kids make the choice, they're going to say, "I want the big orange one," and you may end up living with a furry cow for fifteen years. Decide if you want a big or small pet, a male or female, one with long or short fur.

Go to an animal shelter if you want an inexpensive, mixed-breed dog and save its life by adopting it. Get a dog magazine, call a national dog association, talk to a veterinarian, or go to a dog show to find out where to get a pure-bred puppy. Pet shops are okay if you are experienced in picking a healthy animal and if its family history is unimportant to you.

A healthy puppy has clear, bright eyes. The teeth should be almost white with pink gums. Sometimes there is a natural black-spotted coloring on the gums. This is normal. There should be no liquid or crusty discharge from the animal's eyes, ears, or nose. Its coat must be loose, supple, and low-lustered (depending on the breed), with no bare patches. If there is one puppy that is obviously in bad health, do not pick any animal from that group. Pass them by. Look for unnatural markings or discoloration in the eyes. A young animal with a distended belly may have internal parasites or some other ailment. Do not pick one that is unnaturally fat or thin, or unusually different from the rest of the litter. Watch for continual rubbing of the eyes, ears, or nose. This could be a sign of skin disease, external parasites (mites), or infection. Some are born deaf. Test for deafness by gently clapping your hands behind the puppy and watching for a response.

Nothing is more important than temperament, emotional stability, and normal behavior. Look for a playful yet calm and stable disposition. The shy dog is abnormally afraid of anything unfamiliar and tries to avoid humans, other animals, or change of any kind. Shy behavior involves cringing, cowering, hiding, and defensive aggression. The normal or basic puppy is curious, energetic, playful, and anxious to greet you unless he is ill or has a behavioral problem.

When selecting a puppy for behavior, hold it in your arms with the belly facing up. If the dog submits with ease and pleasure, his temperament is a basic, even one. If he squirms desperately to get away, or whines and whimpers with intensity, he is either aggressive or nervous. If he wets or shivers with fear, he is either shy or timid to the extreme. Children are best matched up with a dog of sound, even temperament. Avoid the puppy that cowers in the corner, no matter how appealing he may be. It can only lead to future behavioral problems.

Who Should Take Care of the Dog

Child/adult dog responsibilities almost always get confused in the turmoil of conflicting points of view about children and dogs. Some parents will not take in a dog unless they make an unworkable bargain that the child assume full responsibility for the totally dependent animal. Conversely, some parents do not allow the child to assume any of the dog chores for fear of the animal harming the child or the child harming the animal.

In reality, neither of these viewpoints are correct. There are some aspects of dog care that should always be handled by an adult, exclusively. However, many activities connected with the dog's health and happiness can and should be the sole province of the younger members of the household.

There are many different circumstances bringing together children and dogs. The most common one is when the child asks for it. Sometimes they beg and plead. Many parents in this situation agree to keeping a dog, with the condition that the child must assume full responsibility for the animal. The child always agrees. Whether this is right or wrong, good or bad, practical or otherwise, is a matter of opinion. Every parent is going to make a personal, subjective decision, no matter who says what.

It is only reasonable and fair that the child who asked for a dog be required to take care of it more than the child who has had the dog thrust upon him or her as a gift. When requesting a dog, few children realize the extent of the effort involved in its care. As time passes, many children become more and more negligent of their dog's needs. A parent's options in this situation are to assume full responsibility themselves; to dispose of the dog (in a humane manner, of course); or to make greater demands on the child. A sensible approach would be to taper the child into the responsibility by gradually introducing the various activities on a one-at-a-time basis. Sooner or later, every child is given some household chores. One or more dog-care chores along with them is not unreasonable and may help strengthen the relationship between dog and child. In addition, it may afford the child a sense of satisfaction and ego gratification. Praise and slight rewards for a job well done reinforce the child's sense of pride in taking care of the dog.

For the sake of both dog and child, parental guidance and supervision are absolutely necessary when it comes to dog care. No matter how much or how little responsibility falls to the child, he or she must be taught what to do. It is definitely a parent's responsibility to instruct and supervise. One way or another, parents are going to be immersed in dog care. When there is more than one child, responsibility for the dog's needs can be shared. Sometimes a puppy is given to only one of several children in a family. Whether this is good or bad depends on the circumstances. One child may love dogs while another does not. If you have two or three children who all love dogs, who all want one, and you give the dog to only one, obviously that's unfair and potential trouble. It is reasonable to give one dog to any number of children. Then the dog is another member of the family, like a new baby, and becomes a family responsibility rather than an individual possession with possible failure lurking in the background.

The following is a schedule for children's dog-care responsibilities. It must be viewed as a guideline only and not taken as the last word on the subject. Remain flexible and do what is possible. Some children will be able to take on more responsibility and some less than what is indicated in the schedule. It is best to follow the dictates of the child in this respect. The schedule has been developed so that the parent might have a general idea of which dog-care responsibilities children can assume at a given age.

Schedule for Children's Dog-Care Responsibilities

Toddlerhood

This period lasts from approximately nine months to three years. So much is happening in a child's development during these months that one would hardly think dog-care responsibilities would be appropriate. Not true. There are some dog-connected activities that provide an ideal outlet for a toddler's boundless curiosity and desire to discover the world. There are no dog chores for a child of this age that can be competently achieved without a parent's assistance. But the rewards for allowing the toddler to participate in the family dog's activities are very great. Self-sufficiency, creative play, a sense of individuality, feelings of competency, and being a part of the family are just some of the benefits derived by a toddler who helps her parents or brothers and sisters take care of their dog.

When a toddler is past eighteen months, he or she is able to help empty the grocery bag and carry the dog's food from the bag to the table. The same applies to the shelf on which it is stored. The simple act of handing you the can or box of dog food may not seem like much, but is certain to make him or her feel truly accomplished.

At two years old a child can help you with other tasks connected with the dog. For example, when you wash the dog's food and water bowls, your assistant can attempt to dry them (if you show him how). It would be a good idea to check the work and point out the moisture he didn't get. Once the bowls are completely dry, both you and the toddler can pour or spoon the dog food and water into them. Caution: Do not allow a toddler to hand the food to the dog or get too close to the feeding area on the floor. Some dogs misinterpret the child's presence at their food and become aggressive. To avoid the possibility of getting bitten, the child should never get too close to the dog while he is being fed or actually eating. It could make him snap, growl, or bite. It can be dangerous with some dogs.

A two-year-old can also help a parent tidy up the dog's area, be it a kennel, a doghouse, or a corner of the kitchen with a blanket on the floor. Minor tasks involving a cleaning cloth or whiskbroom are ideal. You might even give her a turn with the mop. At this age many children love to help out with chores as a way of testing their competency by imitating their parents. It is a rare opportunity to develop in the child the pleasure and gratification of responsibility.

From nine months to three years, children understand so much more than adults realize. This may be because of their limited use of speech. Their powers of comprehension far exceed their desire or ability to use language actively. If you speak slowly and simply, at eye level, a toddler will understand what it is you want him or her to do. Once the request is made, it is up to the parent to take the child by the hand and begin the assignment. Remember, the child is only assisting you and must be instructed and supervised. Once the task has been completed (or seems so to the child), inspect the work and offer your praise and congratulations. Tell the dog what a good job your little girl or boy has done and elicit some enthusiasm from the pet. Dogs get excited when their owners get excited. They quickly perceive human emotions and get caught up in them. It is therefore not difficult to make the dog appear to praise your toddler for a job well done.

Three to Five

Children of this age group may help prepare the dog's meals (although they should not feed the animal directly). They may continue to help clean the dog's utensils, equipment (leashes and collars, etc.), dog's areas, and house areas where the dog has shed fur or knocked things over. During this period most children develop a greater attention span and are capable of more difficult tasks. They are more self-confident and able to exercise greater patience. Language has become fluid and understandable. Children between three and five can take a more dominant position over the dog. This dominance is highly desirable because of the dog's difficulty later in accepting status changes in members of his pack.

Three-to-five-year-old children stand well above the eye level of a medium-sized dog. This is not necessarily threatening to the dog, providing the child's behavior does not indicate a challenge to his position of dominance. Let us not forget that for three years (one-sixth of the average dog's lifetime) the family pet has viewed the young child from infancy to toddlerhood as a puppy or subordinate member of the pack. If the dog has always taken a leader's position in the family, then there may be trouble ahead for a growing child. Even a dog that has been subordinate to other members of the family may feel threatened by the transition of a child's size and behavior as the years pass. In a wolf pack, the alpha wolf (leader) may be forced to step down from his dominant position by a younger and stronger male. But, as one can imagine, it does not happen without a fight.

Although it has not been ascertained scientifically, it is safe to assume that there is a time in the family dog's life when he accepts the fluctuations of pack structure and resigns himself to the idea that there is one less subordinate member in his family. Prior to acceptance, there may be a defensive-aggressive action resulting in a young child's getting bitten. There is no reason why parents cannot prevent this type of incident if they intelligently shape the relationship between dog and child. It is during this period of childhood (three to five) that the preventive measures can be taken.

A child in this age range is still learning from parental example. Therefore, his parents must relate to the dog in a loving but firm tone of voice when giving commands and instructions. The child can be guided to relate in the same manner. Everything must be done to encourage the child to take a leadership position in relationship to the dog, but it must be done gently and as smoothly as possible. If the dog is taken out for a walk, a four- or five-year-old can accompany his parent and even hold the leash for a moment or two. Anything that places the child in a dominant position over the dog is desirable, providing the parent is there to prevent the dog from rebelling. Teach your five-year-old how to hook the leash to the dog's collar before going outdoors. Make that one of his responsibilities, but never without your presence. If the dog has been obedience trained, start teaching your child how to execute the various commands. Remember: a three- to five-year-old is too frail in manner and physical presence to truly dominate the average adult dog.

Take things slowly without expecting too much of the child or the dog. This is merely the beginning of a slow transition in their relationship. It is very encouraging to note that most dogs adore their young family members once they are able to spend time together without adult supervision. That comes later. But a dog and an older child hanging out together is a joyous sight. This is the time to prepare for that time.

Six to Ten

There seems to be general agreement among child experts that the age of six is a difficult one for many children. Six is an age of emotional extremes. A confusing mixture of baby and child, parents often find him quite difficult to handle.

This is a time when a child is breaking away from total dependency on his or her home and parents and is forcing himself or herself to explore the world outside. It is also the time when most children begin formal schooling, which can be an emotional drain. It is probably not a good time to make very many demands in regard to dog care. A six-year-old can be obstinate, easily distracted, and insistent on doing things his or her own way (whether right or wrong). However, the need for a dog's love may be greater than ever. It is probably best to allow a child of six to accept whatever responsibilities he or she can handle for the dog and not push things too far. For the sake of the dog's needs, other members of the family should assume full responsibility for the animal's care until this difficult period is over.

Seven to ten is quite another matter when it comes to dog care. At this age there are few chores connected with a dog that a child cannot accomplish. Still, you must supervise and, at times, assist in various activities, such as grooming procedures, baths, medical treatment. A young child in this age range should not have to take a pet to the veterinarian's office unescorted. It's a good idea for a young dog owner to share that responsibility with a parent. It is a question of the seriousness of the dog's illness in relationship to the degree of sensitivity of the child to such situations. If a dog is extremely sick or near death, it may be a good idea to allow the child to witness those events and procedures leading to euthanasia or natural death. Bearing witness to the truth is a good rule to live by and applies to the unhappy aspects of life as well as any other. It is, of course, a matter of parental discretion.

An eight-, nine-, or ten-year-old is mature enough and strong enough to walk the average dog alone and should be given that responsibility. This may not be true in certain urban areas and certainly does not apply to long walks that turn into hiking excursions. Short walks close to home are an excellent chore for the young dog owner. A child of these years must be instructed about desirable outdoor toilet areas for the dog. Children are often oblivious to the amenities of being a good neighbor and might allow their dogs to relieve themselves on lawns, sidewalks, or building walls. This must be discouraged.

Children between the ages of six and ten may now participate in feeding the family pet but must still exercise caution with dogs that are extremely territorial. If this type of dog is used to being fed by the adults of the household, it may become snappish if the food is handled by younger members of the family. In the natural state, the entire wolf pack participates in the hunt for food. But once the kill is made, the dominant members of the pack eat first while the subordinate members wait their turn and take what's left. This is especially true in the winter, when game is scarce. Unless the family dog has come to accept a child as a dominant figure, it is going to be uneasy about that child being near its food. It takes a while for the dog to understand that the child is not taking—but rather giving—the food. You must remain present as the child feeds the dog. Ideally, both parent and child together should position the food in its proper place. This helps the dog to fully accept the child's shift in status from subordinate to dominant pack member.

Another responsibility for children of this age is the dog's need for exercise, which does not mean just walking the dog. Most walks are for toilet purposes, anyway. There is probably no greater exercise for a dog than a good romping play period with children. Every house or apartment offers its own set of physical limitations on this kind of play. But there is always room enough for some degree of physical play between a child and a dog, and it is such a desirable activity that it is well worth the noise and inconvenience. Here is a responsibility that every child will enjoy and benefit from at the same time. Both dog and child are not only exercised but enjoy the development of strong bonds of friendship as they interact. They will play and then they will relax and enjoy each other's company in a way that few adults can experience. A ball, a stick, a bone, or a cardboard box are almost all that is needed for this purpose. Of course, the child must be guided so that the dog is not hurt or overstimulated. Sometimes a dog really wants to call it quits, but the child continues, unaware of the animal's exhaustion or oncoming irritability. This problem is easily solved by parents setting a time limit on the play-exercise period and also by confining it to one room.

Eleven and Twelve

This stage of childhood is referred to as preadolescence. Many physical and mental developments are taking place at the same time and they often conflict with one another, such as the dependencies of childhood clashing with the drive toward independence. Large, overpowering emotions can erupt from eleven- and twelve-year-olds. Sometimes those feelings are not fully expressed, but just seething under the surface. Emotions range from one extreme to another, and one can see joy and despair, elation and dejection from day to day, or sometimes from hour to hour. Children of this age are often moody, suspicious, or irritable. Because this is in part a difficult period for adult and child alike, the pleasures of dog ownership can be especially beneficial. Being totally responsible for the needs and desires of a dog offers for the child, the immeasurable reward of self-confidence, and for the parent, an understanding of his or her child's competence. With the exception of the dog's medical needs (veterinary examinations, home-nursing procedures, and home diagnoses) and, to some extent, obedience training, an eleven- or twelve-year-old child can assume all responsibilities for a dog.

The right dog with the right child can offer the ideal private relationship that does not have to be shared. With luck and parental skill, an eleven- or twelve-year-old might just find in a dog the middle ground between emotional turmoil and family love. It is important here to consider the well-being of the dog. Therefore it must be made clear that along with the comfort that the dog brings, there must also come a dedication to its care. If the child cannot enter into such an agreement, it is best for all concerned to forgo the relationship and allow the animal to become the family pet. However, it is difficult to imagine a dog not being able to burrow beneath the barriers of preadolescence and relate lovingly to any child.

Thirteen to Fifteen

Probably the most important liberty for the early teenage child is the freedom of choice. Finding out what he or she prefers and allowing for independent decisions in regard to dog ownership is essential. Allow for the inconsistencies between declarations of independence and quiet requests for money and other kinds of assistance. Once your teenager takes on the burden of dog care, don't be surprised if a little neglect or abdication of some responsibilities creep in along the edges. Discussions and adjustments of dog-care responsibilities will probably be in order. The many benefits of a relationship between a human and a dog have all been stated before and apply to a greater degree with a teenager.

A girl or a boy between thirteen and fifteen years old can take on any and all aspects of dog care, providing he or she understands that the dog's very life is in his or her hands. Probably the most worthwhile and rewarding responsibility for a child in this age range is teaching the dog basic obedience. There is much to be learned through this activity by dog and child. With the help of a competent dog obedience book or classroom instruction, both dog and child learn to bring order from confusion and chaos. For the dog, there is the security of affirming his position in the family pack order. For the child, dog obedience offers lessons in leadership, self-discipline, and responsibility.

Dogs and Other Dogs

Living with more than one dog can be wonderful or less than wonderful. Despite the fact that humans control the day-to-day destiny of their family pets, all domestic dogs have instinctive aspects of their behavior that cannot be suppressed. Much of this behavior is seen in connection with other dogs. It is essential for pet owners to understand that dogs experience our shared world from a totally different perspective. That perspective is so different and unique from the human experience that to be unaware of it is to not understand your dog at all. How can anyone understand, control, and enjoy a dog if that dog's way of relating to other dogs is a complete mystery?

An important aspect of dog behavior has to do with sensory perceptions, particularly as they apply to relations between dogs. It can be said that human understanding of the world is an intellectual one with an emphasis on visual perception. This is not the case for the domestic dog. There is no evidence that dogs intellectually evaluate anything about the environment in which they find themselves or about other dogs they encounter. Part of the reason for the incredible adaptability of domestic dogs is their willingness to accept conditions as they are and make the necessary adjustments to survive. It can also be said that visual perception is probably one of the least developed sensory perceptors that dogs possess. With limited intellectual capacity and mediocre vision, the dog must rely on other means for maintaining himself in a sometimes dangerous and difficult world.

The average dog sees human society from approximately twenty-five inches above the floor. By getting on all fours and crouching, you may begin to understand more about a dog's-eye view of his home and surrounding terrain. In the human home, the dog has no choice but to learn to communicate in order to satisfy his needs. Eye contact, touching, and vocalizing must all be put into play if the dog wants its dinner or to be let out for toileting, etc. Unfortunately, these are the dog's least natural abilities and require great effort to utilize adequately. However, in the dog's natural setting, conditions are quite different, especially when dogs communicate with each other.

Vision is not the most important means of communication between dogs. Even so, the sight of another dog is usually the first perception, despite its limitations. Canine sight relies upon sound and smell to complete the visual message to the brain. Visual proficiency varies from breed to breed and sometimes from dog to dog within some breeds. The best example is the difference between gazehounds (swift dogs that hunt by sight) such as Whippets, Afghan Hounds, and Greyhounds, and scent hounds (slower dogs that hunt by smell), such as Bloodhounds, Basset Hounds and Beagles. When comparing the visual capacity of dogs and humans, there are two aspects to be considered. The dog's peripheral vision is almost twice that of the human's; however, the human's ability to focus sharply is much greater than the dog's. These are important differences. The result is that a dog is acutely sensitive to motion and perceives it before humans can. But he must rely on sound and smell to know what he has just seen. Because dogs are essentially prey seekers, they respond on a hair-trigger mechanism at the first sight of strange and sudden motion. This accounts for their chasing other dogs, cats, cars, and bicycles, impulsively running out of the house, and a long list of negative behaviors.

Dogs can hear better than humans but not quite as well as cats. They can hear sounds that we cannot, and can listen for a familiar footstep long before it comes within human earshot. The so-called Galton whistle or silent dog whistle is not silent at all. It is pitched at a frequency too high for the human ear but quite clear to the canine or feline ear. Another way in which a dog's hearing differs from human hearing is in its better sense of rhythm. A dog can tell if the beat of a metronome changes from a hundred to ninety-six beats a minute. A human can only detect this when timing the beats with a stopwatch. This is an ability that is extremely useful when hunting for food animals or when confronting natural enemies. The dog not only has sensitive hearing but is able to determine breathing rhythms and possibly the quantity of footsteps and at what speed they are moving.

In dealing with friend, foe, or prey, the dog's front line of defense is the olfactory receptor within his nose—in other words, his smelling apparatus. All mammals possess an olfactory mechanism under a membrane. In humans it is about the size of a postage stamp. Under the membrane are thousands of nerve fibers terminating in olfactory hairs. The various scents (in gas form) pass over these nerve fibers and send messages to the brain concerning the nature of the scent. In the average dog the olfactory membrane, when spread out, is fifty times greater than that of the human membrane. However, a dog's nose is not necessarily more sensitive than a human's. The dog excels in the variety of smells he can detect.

In the receptor area of the dog's olfactory mechanism, the receptors are interspersed with glandular cells which secrete a mucous substance. The odor molecules of one odor are thought to separate differentially in the mucus and therefore cause different spatial stimulation of the receptor field than other odors. This is the physiology of odor reception.

The key to a dog's perception of his world lies in his smelling abilities. Scent posting and scent perception are among the main activities of all dogs. Through this unique set of mechanisms and behaviors a dog seeks and finds food, obtains a mate, claims territory, fights for his rights and his life (if necessary), mates, tends the young, and maintains an instinctive integrity within his social structure. All of this depends largely on his ability to use his incredible nose. When a dog sees another dog, his smelling apparatus immediately goes to work, probing for information and various signals. His hearing and taste also come into play, but the dog's behavior from that point on is very much influenced by what his nose tells him. In addition, dogs have an uncanny ability to catalog and remember thousands of odors and their associations with people, animals, places, and events. One could call it "scent memory." The greatest of the dog's smelling talents is its capacity to discriminate one odor from hundreds of odors, from great distances and over long periods of time. These are the abilities that make it possible to use them as rescue dogs, trailing dogs, bomb detection dogs, and drug detection dogs. It is necessary for the dog owner to understand the nature of animal senses and how they differ in order of importance for dogs. There have been many cases of dogs losing their eyesight and still managing efficiently with the help of the more important sense of hearing and smell. The order of importance—smell, hearing, and then sight—helps the pet owner appreciate how the dog perceives the world he lives in. It is particularly essential when living under the same roof with two or more dogs.

When two dogs first meet, they either examine one another by smelling and licking each other or display a unique body language from a safe distance. The result may be that they will fight, mate, play, or simply walk away. When dog meets dog, one of four issues arise: 1) dominance; 2) territory; 3) sex; or 4) play. In most cases the meeting will involve a combination of two or more of these issues.

Male dogs are more likely to fight each other than females. When examining and smelling each other, a fight may ensue if one or the other's odor indicates a high level of testosterone (usually in a young or adolescent dog). Quite often, the examination never takes place and is replaced by aggressive body language that is mostly bluff. The two dogs may communicate their competition through their body position, facial expression, and vocalization. A challenging dog assumes a threatening posture of erect head, fixed stare, pricked ears, taut muscles, stiffened legs, erect but usually still tail, and the appearance of a general increase in body size. Sometimes the dog's fur stands up and away from the body, creating the impression of more bulk and height. Many dogs then turn sideways to further impress their opponents with a show of even more body mass. The teeth may be displayed and a low, throaty growl may be produced. At the sound of the growl an attack is probably imminent and the owners of both dogs should leave the area quickly. That is how dogs respond to each other as strangers or competitors.

Still, all dogs are social creatures, due to inherited instincts that are drawn from pack behavior. The wolf pack is essentially a small family of wolves living together in a very specific social organization. If your dog is left alone much of the time, as many pet dogs are, he is living out an existence similar to that of the lone wolf. It is an unnatural and unhappy physical and mental state for a dog. A lone wolf is one who has become too old or too sick to fulfill his destiny within the pack order. He is an outcast and does not last very long in the remote wilderness. Because of their need for pack structure, dogs do not thrive at their best when left alone most of the time. Although there is never one cure-all answer, a possible solution for this is the introduction of another dog into the environment.

There are many variables involved, and matching the right dog with the right companion has a great deal to do with the temperament of the dog and how social he is. It is best when the dogs are of the same sex, to avoid the problems of unwanted mating and pregnancies (unless one or more of the dogs are neutered). The new dog could be a puppy, providing the established dog is not too old.

A new puppy will have no problem living with the domination of a larger animal. Because of their age and size differences, the established dog will have the upper hand, for a while. The two dogs will immediately work out their respective status differences in the household. A few antagonistic encounters between two new dogmates is to be expected. It is how they work out who is top dog. Unless they are violent, these encounters should be permitted. They usually end with the small dog rolling over on his back with his belly in the air. He may even piddle. These are gestures of submission and acknowledgment of the other dog's dominance. From then on there is usually peace in the family.

While a young puppy might require more attention at first, there is no reason why the older pet cannot be given reassuring pats on the head, some extra soothing words, or a few additional minutes of play and attention. When introducing a new dog into the house, it is important to have separate food and water dishes for each pet and to feed them in opposite corners of the room to make certain that neither pet feels compelled to protect his food or compete for it. Watch out that the older, larger dog does not take the younger dog's food from him.

If the older pet is a senior citizen, the addition of a youngster to the family can have some stressful results. The competition may place too much emotional and physical strain on the older dog. It depends on the temperament of the older dog and how advanced in years he is. A very old dog must be spared the extreme change of a new dog in his life.

There are those who feel that dogs never seek the society of other dogs to ease their loneliness or boredom, but rather prefer to have the human owner all to themselves. This is the exception rather than the rule. That point of view seems to go against the obvious logic of pack behavior. Although dogs are not wolves, they do share this proclivity for a social existence with other dogs. The problem between two dogs—particularly two males (or two females)—is one of domination and subordination. The matter of territory is one that has to do with dogs of different families or packs. Two grown male dogs will, in all likelihood, have to have a scrap in order to determine the dominant and subordinate roles. No dog is too young or too old for obedience training. If your dogs are under control, you can be certain that an occasional scrap will bring no physical harm to either animal. Allow the dogs to play with one another for ten or fifteen minutes at a time and make sure they are gentle with each other. If it sounds or looks like it is getting out of hand, chances are it is. Separate the dogs, give them each a food treat and keep them away from each other for a while.

A new puppy should be constantly socialized with new situations, new people, and other dogs. This will allow for the introduction of an additional dog in the house if it becomes desirable.

Dogs and Cats

Although dogs and cats sharing the same home develop meaningful relationships, they do it in species-specific ways. Contrary to popular mythology, dogs and cats can, for the most part, live quite well together, sharing territory, food, and human contact. However, one must develop a realistic view of dog and cat biology and behavior to enjoy the dynamic interaction between the two species.

What domestic dogs and cats have in common is a dependency created by human indulgence and kindness. Emotional and physical dependency created by humans is what allows dogs and cats to live together, sharing the same home and the same humans. This is the result of many generations of domesticity. It promotes the ability of cats and dogs to live together, sharing the same home and the same set of human guardians, despite the vast differences in their natural behavior. Human affection has created dependencies in their pets that have resulted in a parent/child-type relationship. Consequently, house pets have lost many of their adult, wild instincts and have remained in a sort of adolescent state. The best part is that dogs and cats often become totally devoted to each other and develop relationships that are as meaningful as any that exist between humans. But this can only happen in the right environment, with the correct set of circumstances. One could argue that a canine and feline have no choice but to get along, once thrown together, and therefore must find a way to make it work. To some degree this is true. However, anyone living in this human/animal configuration knows there is more to it than simple accommodation.

Living with dogs and cats together is an enjoyable and civilizing experience. It is also a fascinating experiment with nature. When two totally different kinds of animals are thrown together and make adjustments so that survival is assured and the fulfillment of animal destiny is realized, it can be an overwhelming experience.

Cats and dogs are quite different from a behavioral point of view, but their differences are not based on one being a more dominant animal than the other. Quite the contrary, they are both species that develop a dominant/subordinate order within the societies of their own species. As discussed earlier, dog behavior is similar to wolf behavior. Pack structure is the most important aspect of wild behavior for the average dog owner to understand. Wolves most often travel and thrive in packs or loose-knit families consisting of relatives, distant relatives, and occasional non-related individuals. They are led by a dominant wolf who is always the largest, strongest, and most aggressive individual in the pack. Sometimes the pack leader, or alpha wolf, is a female. The pack itself develops a social order of rank based on dominance and subordination. This fact is of vital importance to dog owners. Domestic dogs, like wolves, develop social attachments based on a pecking order and, for the most part, adhere to it quite rigidly, except on those rare occasions when the alpha is challenged.

This social lifestyle is genetically organized into their behavior. When a dog is taken to its new home, the human family substitutes for the more natural pack. This is true even if the family consists of one human and one or two other companion animals. From the dog's point of view, the range and territory belonging to the pack (or human family) is the apartment or house, with or without acreage. That is why dogs take to family life so naturally. A young dog, even an aggressive one, will quickly sort out in his mind who is dominant and who is not within the pack structure of the human family (and that includes cats as well).

Cats, on the other hand, are not animals oriented to a social order, at least not one that we commonly recognize. Most wild cats are solitary creatures who come together and stay together for mating and rearing their young. At all other times both males and females live separately within their exclusive ranges and territories, with the exception of lions who live in prides (a kind of pack). This singular lifestyle in the wild is the foreshadowing behavior of most domestic cats. It is why they appear to be independent and often indifferent to human pampering. Over the generations of domestic pampering, humans have treated their pet cats like human children or, more significantly, like small kittens. This has encouraged cats to behave in an infantile or adolescent manner. Thus, we have a feline creature that wants to be fed on schedule, groomed, played with, and given large quantities of affection. How unlike their image, not to mention their wild "grownup" cousins.

When one witnesses two or more cats living together and getting along, it is because they are adhering to an instinct to sort themselves out in some social order of top cat and low cat. However, in cat societies, that can change suddenly and even frequently. It is based on the behavior of shifting social rank in an uncontrolled mating situation that can be witnessed in any backyard.

What domestic dogs and cats have in common is dependency created by human indulgence and kindness. Emotional and physical dependency created by humans is what allows dogs and cats to live together, sharing the same home and the same set of human guardians. Although dogs and cats are not natural enemies, neither are they natural friends. They too often compete for space, food, water, human affection, and attention.

Male dogs that are highly territorial, especially the terriers and some of the working breeds, are very dominant in nature and quite assertive. The same is true of some females. However, cats, too, can be dominant in their behavior. A dominant dog stakes out specific objects and locations as territorial boundaries and can get quite ugly about them. Most common are food and water bowls, sleeping quarters, a special corner of a room, or even a person. Although some cats also prize these objects and locations, they will rarely fight over them unless it is with another cat. Cats become more assertive about pathways leading to favored locations, attention from favored individuals, food treats not on the daily menu, play objects, catnip, and sex objects.

Over the years the two animals sort things out, for the most part, and learn to stay away from one another's sensitive areas. Many a dog has received an embedded cat claw in its nose because it went that extra step. There can be no doubt that a large, aggressive dog will gain the upper hand over a cat, providing the cat is caught off guard. But heaven help a dog that backs a mature cat into a corner and means business. In the end, the dog may win out, but it will have cost a terrible physical price. This rarely happens, because in the early stages of a dog/cat relationship one takes full measure of the other and behaves with common sense.

The most successful dog/cat relationships are developed when the animals are introduced to each other as puppies and kittens. A very young kitten will imprint on a grown dog with greater ease than a young dog on a grown cat. Because there are so many variables here, one must allow for all kinds of exceptions to this rule.

Dogs and cats have needs that sometimes blend and sometimes clash at different periods of their lives and create the shifting sands of dominance and subordination. A teething dog or a cat in heat should be separated from the other animal until he is behaving normally. Terriers and most hunting dogs should not be allowed near newborn kittens, as they are apt to mistake them for rodents or prey animals. Some dogs who are avowed cat haters will often develop a loving relationship with the family cat while still hating them as a species and attacking strays. A lactating queen (mother cat) will viciously attack a curious dog who gets too close to a young litter of kittens. An assertive, unaltered male cat would not have the subordinate manner necessary to get along with a large, territorial canine.

A cat and dog living in the same human environment must compete for space, food, water, and attention. The conduct of the human family will certainly help to shape the relationship.

Here are some guidelines:

1) Establish a well-defined dog/cat system within your house. Give each animal an area exclusively its own. Place their "dens" or "lairs" as far apart as possible and at different heights. For a dog, a carton with a blanket placed in the corner of a room or basement is sufficient, although a wire dog crate is best. If possible, give the cat a territory on a higher level, such as a wicker basket on the second floor or a food bowl on a mantel.

2) Feed your pets at different times and in different places. Special attention such as baths and other grooming procedures should be given when the other pet is not present.

3) Obedient pets are more likely to live in harmony with each other than those without organized behavioral responses to human commands. Try obedience training for both animals. You can buy a manual and work with your pet on your own, or enroll the dog in an obedience school.

4) If possible, bring animals together when they are young. The most successful dog/cat relationships are developed when the animals are introduced as puppies and kittens. However, a young kitten will attach itself to a grown dog and develop a subordinate relationship to it. Introducing a puppy to a grown cat is more difficult and requires a great deal of patience.

In most dog/cat households one animal rarely wants what is important to the other, and that is what makes it all work. Depending on temperament, early socialization, obedience training, and a loving environment, most dogs will make some sort of peace with even the most impudent of cats.

Cats and dogs. Pets and people. They're all in this thing together. Sometimes a dog rules the roost. Sometimes a cat. Sometimes both. It is all very much influenced by human behavior. Bear in mind that the first Love Boat was the Ark.

5

GETTING
YOUR DOG
UNDER CONTROL

The only way your dog is ever going to behave properly in all important situations is if he is obedience trained. Dog training is not a luxury, it is a necessity. Big dogs, little dogs, pure-breeds and mutts, they all need to be trained. Dog training is a means of teaching a dog how to live in a human environment. It is a step-by-step, systematic method of organizing a dog's responses to authority that directs him toward obeying various, but quite specific, commands. This procedure gives humans and dogs a satisfying and workable relationship. Most people train their dogs so that they may have an enjoyable relationship based on mutual love and trust. This is best accomplished with the help of a professional dog trainer.

Although having your dog trained by a professional is costly, it may be less expensive in the larger picture when considering aggravation and a long, drawn-out period of dissatisfaction and possible destructive behavior. There are many professional dog trainers available throughout the United States. They can be easily found in the classified pages of your phone directory or through recommendations from veterinarians and fellow dog owners.

Few are as intimately acquainted with dog behavior and how to alter it as are professional dog trainers. As professionals, their opinions are based on a knowledge of dogs that few possess. Building upon an inherent or intuitive understanding of animals and a personal magnetism that commands the attention of most dogs, professional dog trainers commit themselves to the study and acquisition of the techniques and skills involved, serving an apprenticeship with accomplished professionals and accumulating intensive working experience.

Because professional dog trainers are committed to preventing and helping to solve the problems that arise between humans and their dogs, they have become an essential element connecting dog behavior and human behavior.

Expert dog trainers work directly with canine behavior and temperament every day of their lives. At times they place themselves at personal risk in order to make life safer and happier for people and the dogs they love. They relate to hundreds of dogs each year. Their professional judgment in matters relating to dogs and society is invaluable.

Still, you can always choose less expensive obedience classes (conducted privately or by animal shelters and humane societies), join obedience clubs (The American Kennel Club has lists of them), or try it yourself with the help of a book such as this one. Here is an understanding of what dog training is, how it works, and why it works. It could help you select a trainer or a method of training.

A professional trainer or a knowledgeable pet owner must have a grasp of basic dog behavior to successfully train a dog. Otherwise, the situation becomes one of psychological, emotional, and even physical conflict. The objectives should be to first bond with the dog in a loving relationship, then establish your dominance in that relationship, and finally begin dog training. Many aspects of dog behavior are not considered acceptable to humans even though they are natural for dogs. Dog training is the only way to teach a dog how to live in a human environment without losing his home. (For an understanding of dog behavior please refer to Chapter Two, "The Canine Response.") Once you understand the basics of dog behavior, you are ready to effectively use training techniques that enhance your relationship, rather than harm it.

As previously stated, dog behavior is similar to wolf behavior, which has been studied by researchers for decades. Dogs and wolves form social attachments and live in groups known as packs. They require a leader. They claim territory and create a den in the center of it where they rest, sleep, and eat.

Although wolves and dogs behave similarly in many ways, their similarities differ in degree of intensity and aggression. Because wolves are wild animals, they are far less trusting than dogs. Dogs have shared their lot with humans for thousands of years and this has modified their behavior from what it was in the wild. For example, an alpha wolf is an aggressive animal that leads its pack and often asserts its dominance with violent threats or attacks. One must not dominate a dog in the same manner that a wolf pack leader would when dealing with an insubordinate pack member. That would create an undesirable pet.

The pack instinct in dogs and wolves creates a desire in them to work as team members hunting for food, maintaining pack integrity, and mating and rearing cubs. Pack instinct establishes the need to be with other creatures. When living as pets, dogs transfer this need to humans. The human family is viewed as a substitute pack by the dog, even if there is only one person. This explains why dogs are constant and loyal companions.

As stated in Chapter Two, the survival of wolves (and dogs) in the wild depends on leadership. An alpha wolf or pack leader is one that asserts itself and takes that position, usually by force. A "leader of the pack" becomes established along with other dominant and subordinate pack members who sort themselves out in some order of rank. The need for leadership is primary if a pack is to survive. Every dog requires that someone assume a leadership position. Your pet will accept the position of command if no one else will. However, dogs readily accept leadership from those with dominant personalities or who behave with some degree of authority. Once you assume the position of leader, your dog will accept it for life.

Dogs, like wolves, require safety areas for resting, eating and sleeping. These are aspects of their territory, the most important place being the den which in the wild is often a cave, a tunnel, or a hollowed-out log. In our homes the dog may consider the entire house as the den, or it may simply be a corner, a dog bed, or a dog crate.

These are the most important aspects of dog behavior as they pertain to dog training. With this information one can better decide which dog training methods compliment the animal's natural tendencies and which contradict them.

Why Train Your Dog?

Believe it or not, by training your dog you make him happier because of the emotional security it gives him. It also makes you happier because it eliminates the most common complaint: "My dog never listens to me." If a dog is not obedient he is not living in a way that is normal for him. If your pet was living in a dog pack he would be under the control of a pack leader and others of higher rank. All dogs, whether they live in nature or in your home, thrive on the concept of leaders and followers. Behaving according to the rules of pack order is normal for a dog. It promotes survival and prosperity. By training your dog you provide him with a leader, and that definitely makes him happier.

Dogs, of course, do not "listen" to their owners because they do not understand the spoken language of humans. Long sentences have no meaning to animals. Emotional expression and dog training are the only languages available to you. Dog training involves short spoken commands, a specific tone of voice, hand signals, body language, and various techniques with a leash and training collar. When we use the term dog training we are talking about obedience which is an acceptable term when referring to dogs. You command, and the dog obeys. Training a dog requires that his trainer learns to become the animal's leader. This activity will most definitely improve the dog's perception of you as his leader and, as a side benefit, develop your leadership qualities in general.

It is important, however, to understand that leadership has nothing to do with being a drill sergeant or a high school valedictorian. It is the ability to be responsible, to make decisions, to give commands, and risk failure. If you attend a dog show, watch the professional dog handlers. They are masterful but not abusive. They do not speak loudly or harshly to the dogs. What exists is an immediate communication between dog and human. The human knows what he or she expects from the dog and that gives the dog self-confidence. In the show ring, obedience training is not really a factor. It is the crystal-clear dominant-subordinate relationship that helps achieve the blue ribbon. That is a goal worth going for.

The Truth About Dog Training

In dog training, people lead and dogs follow. To accomplish this you must establish a relationship based on love, kindness, and leadership. Learn to give authoritative commands with insistence, patience, and understanding. Whether your dog is young or old, big or small, you must decide whether to train him yourself or hire a professional to do the job. If you decide to train the dog yourself, you can do it with the information presented here. Even if you hire a professional, the information provided in this chapter will be useful to help you understand what the trainer is doing with your dog. There is no such thing as having your dog trained without your participation. It is essential that you, too, are trained to handle the dog and give the obedience commands that have been taught. If you already live with a grown dog and he isn't trained, now is the time to start. It is never too late to train your dog.

It is essential that all members of your family take a dominant position over the dog. Of course, no one should be allowed to be physically or emotionally abusive. That prevents the puppy from developing into a normal, happy dog. For example, it is harmful to tower over a small dog or handle him roughly. Neither should anyone point a threatening finger at the dog when scolding him. The hands must only be used for expressions of affection and for giving command signals. Hollering and shouting along with physical punishment are useless as training techniques. Being dominant over the family dog does not mean you shouldn't be playful and happy in your day-to-day activities. When you bond with your dog your attitude toward him should be as loving as it is fun. You can be the one in charge and still be cheerful and affectionate. All dogs need to feel that they are accepted members of the pack. That is why they will strive to earn your approval. Obedience training is based on the dog's acceptance of the human's position of dominance and the animal's desire to please. After you teach your dog an obedience command, praise him for executing the command properly (each and every time) and correct him when he does not. That definitely gives you the position of authority. The most important dog training tool you have is the concept of praise and correction.

Approval and Disapproval

Approval is given with *praise*. Your dog must always be rewarded for performing properly, obeying your command (once he has learned it), and for doing the right thing. Because most dogs thrive on their owners' approval your enthusiastic praise means a lot and communicates to him that he was "a good dog." Praise is an extremely valuable teaching tool in dog training. Most dog trainers believe that verbal praise is sufficient reward. However, some trainers believe in rewarding a dog that performs properly with a small food treat. There is some disagreement among dog trainers about this. However, all agree that an affectionate pat on the body works well as an added reward providing the dog is not hyper-energetic. Do not hold back on your enthusiasm when praising your dog unless he is highly excitable, in which case it is best to be a bit more subdued. For example, Golden Retrievers must be praised calmly with no petting; English Setters and Basset Hounds must be praised lavishly.

It is of great importance to understand that every time

you praise your dog, you reinforce the action he took just before the reward was given. In effect, it is a teaching technique. Verbally praising your dog with or without an affectionate pet can be good or bad. If the dog did the right thing then praising him helps him learn to obey you at all times. If he barked at someone and you say in a sweet-sounding voice, "Okay, Prince. No more," the dog feels rewarded for barking and will do it again. Rewarding bad behavior also happens when you try to calm a dog or soothe him after he did something wrong. Do not teach your dog bad behavior by praising him for it. Praise is one of the basics tools of dog training. You must use it properly.

Disapproval is given with *corrections*. When a dog refuses to obey a command, or when he misbehaves, he has earned your disapproval and must be corrected. A correction can be a jerk of the leash that is attached to a training collar and is referred to as a *corrective jerk* by some dog trainers. It is the most effective means of communicating to a dog that his previous action or inaction was wrong. When administering a leash correction you must also say, "NO," in a firm tone of voice. A correction can also be a firm "NO" without the jerk of the leash. Corrections give a mild, negative signal to a dog and communicate your disapproval.

Another method for correcting a dog is to create a loud, startling sound accompanied by a firm, "NO." Make your own noisemaker by putting pennies inside an empty soda can. When the dog is in the act of misbehaving, shake the can vigorously and say "NO" in a loud, firm tone of voice.

Never use corrections unwisely or inhumanely. Do not jerk the leash too hard. You must never hurt your dog. Even harsh verbal reprimands can be abusive and inhumane. Abusive treatment teaches nothing to your dog and very often prevents him from learning anything. Corrections are simply a means of communicating your disapproval and that the dog did the wrong thing. Do not mistake the idea of corrections for punishments. When you hit a dog he may become cowed but not really trained. It is difficult to predict how a dog will respond to punishment. Some dogs may punish you back by snapping or biting. You would never punish a student for learning slowly or for forgetting the previous day's lesson. A good teacher may firmly tell a student his answer was wrong, but will not yank him across the room or call him a dummy. The same applies in dog training.

If you learn when and how to praise or correct your dog effectively, you will have at your fingertips the primary means of communicating with him. Once you learn how to give commands, praise, and corrections you will feel confident in what you are doing and your dog will know he is loved and cared for.

The Requirements for Successful Dog Training

1) Develop a loving relationship with your dog. This is called *bonding*.

2) Read Chapter Two of this book and learn the basics of dog behavior.

3) Read Chapter Three of this book in order to determine your dog's temperament so that you can adjust the training techniques to your dog's personality. Use common sense. If your dog is hyper-sensitive, shy, or timid he must be corrected gently. If he is stubborn or somewhat aggressive you must be more dominant in correcting him.

Extremely aggressive dogs can be dangerous and are probably best trained by a professional.

4) Train your dog to obey the commands that are outlined in the remainder of this chapter.

The Obedience Commands Taught in This Chapter

· **SIT.** The dog will assume a sitting posture on command. The dog's body is upright with his front paws standing straight as his rear weight rests on his haunches.

· **HEEL.** The dog must walk when given the command and carefully pace himself so that he never pulls ahead or lags behind. He is on the left side of his owner with his head approximately next to the left knee.

· **HEEL-SIT.** When walking in HEEL the dog will respond to a stop by going into the SIT position. The dog stops every time the trainer does and sits without being commanded to do so.

· **STAY.** (SIT-STAY or DOWN-STAY) after being given the proper verbal command and hand signal the dog must hold his position until he is released by his owner. He should look straight ahead and move very little.

· **DOWN.** On command the dog lowers his entire body to the ground or the floor. Although he is completely relaxed, his head remains erect as he looks forward in anticipation of your next command. The dog's front paws are stretched out in front of him forming two parallel straight lines. His rear paws are holding his resting body weight.

· **THE RECALL.** The owner uses a precise verbal command and a hand signal so that the dog stops what he is doing, runs to the one who has called him, and places himself in a SIT position when he reaches his destination. Some trainers refer to this command as COME WHEN CALLED.

Objectives

When training your dog the objective is to get a very specific response to each command on a consistent basis. The elements of dog training as outlined in this chapter will help you achieve this. Dog training is about teaching your dog what you expect of him and then learning how to communicate what you want. The first part of the process is to teach the dog the mechanics of a command. This involves the use of praise and corrections. A reward is verbal praise from you. It is given every time the dog executes a command properly.

IMPORTANT: Rewards must be given after every correction. The purpose of praising a dog *after* a correction is to reassure him that he did the right thing by finally complying with your command. This reinforces the teaching process.

The second part of the process is to diligently practice what you have taught the dog every day until you are sure he knows how to fully obey the command. Some dogs are slower or more resistant than others and may frustrate you. Be patient and do not lose your temper. Use a gentle sounding voice but give your commands with authority, especially with stubborn or mildly aggressive dogs. Do not be heavy-handed. Although training time is not play time, you do not have to be oppressive. Coax a sensitive or shy dog instead of bearing down on him. Put an upbeat sound in your voice and never allow anger or hysteria to take over.

Remember, the first step is to teach the mechanics of a command before demanding obedience. Never correct your dog for failing to obey before you are certain he understands how to execute a command. If he fails to obey you it is probably because he hasn't gotten the hang of it yet.

The Leather Leash and Training Collar

The Training Collar. This essential training tool is commonly known as a *choke collar*. Do not be misled by the ominous-sounding name. The word *choke* does not really apply because the collar does not perform in that manner. The metal training collar is a short length of chain made of steel or polished aluminum. Its links are small and should be welded together for maximum strength. At each end of the collar is a large ring. By properly looping the chain through one of the large rings you form a slip knot that is wide enough to slide over the dog's head. Be certain the collar is on properly. The clip of the leash attaches to the outstanding large ring so that both dog and trainer are ready for a workout. Like any slip knot the chain will tighten around the dog's neck when the leash is pulled gently. When this is done the dog experiences a mild sensation. If the word "NO" always accompanies this mild sensation the dog will learn that he has not performed properly. Thus, the training collar becomes an extremely important communicative tool.

The collar must be placed around the animal's neck properly so that the operation of the slip knot is smooth. When the chain is tightened around the dog's neck it must remain tight for only an instant and then slide smoothly to its loose, hanging state. This is important if the dog is to avoid any pain. The metal training collar is not recommended for puppies, small and fragile dogs, or dogs with a long, silky coat (to avoid damaging the hair coat). It is best to get a nylon training collar for dogs of these descriptions.

When purchasing a training collar it is important to get the right size. Measure the diameter of your dog's neck and buy a chain or nylon training collar that is three inches longer than the neck size. The leash is meant to snap onto the out ring.

The Leather Leash. A six-foot leash is precisely what is needed in this dog training course. It will be used in almost every training command and allows for the exact distance required in many of the teaching techniques. This length is especially important when teaching SIT and RECALL. A leash made of leather is what is recommended most, but a canvas training leash is adequate. The leather is more durable and easier to spot when it wears down and is ready to break. The leather leash also avoids hurting the dog's chest or your hand when administering a leash correction.

When purchasing a leather leash you will be confronted with a wide variety of widths to choose from. Naturally, a dog's size will determine how wide the leash should be. However, five-eighths of an inch width is best for most dogs.

Placing the Collar and Leash Around the Dog's Neck

Let the collar hang straight down by holding it with your left hand by the large ring of either end. Take the bottom ring with your right hand and pull some of the chain through it. Next, allow the remainder of the chain to fall through the bottom ring so that it forms a slip knot, resembling a miniature lasso.

The lasso portion of the collar goes over the dog's neck with the ring in your left hand, pointing away from his right side. Once around his neck the collar must tighten around the dog's throat when pulled and release smoothly and instantly when released.

You know you are placing the collar on properly when you slip it over the dog's head and it forms the letter "P" around his neck. You know it is incorrect if the training collar resembles the number "9" on the left and the number "6" on the right. If this is the case it will not tighten and release as it should. With the dog facing you, place the collar on him so the ring will attach to the leash on the left side of his neck. Attach the metal clip of the six-foot leather leash to the outstanding large ring of the collar and you are now ready to begin training your dog.

The Leash Correction

Holding the leash properly. Place the dog in the SIT position, on your left side. Both you and the dog should be facing the same direction. To hold the leash properly, place the thumb of your right hand through the top of the loop of the leash. The lower part of the loop hangs down across your open palm. Next, grab the leash in the middle with your left hand and bring it to the palm of your right hand. The leash should now stretch from the dog's collar, across your knees, with a slight slack in it, leading upward into your right hand. The excess leash dangles by your right leg, forming a large loop. With your right hand held waist-high adjust the length of the leash so that there is no more than the width of your body (allowing for a slight slack). Close the fingers of your right hand around the various strands of the leash that are within your grasp. Your closed fingers, palm facing upward, now have as firm a grip as possible.

Reinforce the grip with the other hand. With the left hand placed directly under the right hand, grasp the various

strands of the leash. The knuckles of the left hand should
be facing upward so that each hand grips the leash in an
opposite direction. You are now in a position to execute
a very firm leash correction. You also have absolute leash
control of the dog's movements. It is almost impossible for
the average dog to bolt from any adult with this grip.

Administering a correction. The dog is in SIT by your
left side. You are both facing the same direction. Both your
hands are holding the leash as described earlier. Your hands
are held slightly below your waist. Jerk the leash quickly toward your right side and return your hands to their
original position immediately. When you jerk the leash the
training collar will tighten around the dog's neck and give
him a mild sensation. Return your hands to their original
position instantly and the collar will automatically loosen,
thus avoiding pain for the animal. Only your arms should
move during the correction and they should head sideways
and slightly upward and back again like a spring. The
action is: jerk and release; jerk and release. The collar
must tighten around the dog's neck and then release in
no longer than a split second. This is very important.

As the collar tightens around the dog's neck say, "NO,"
in a loud, firm tone of voice. If you consistently use the
verbal correction with the leash correction you will eventually not have to jerk the leash at all. A firm "NO" will be
all that is necessary to make any correction or stop the dog
from misbehaving.

Praising the dog enthusiastically with an upbeat tone
after each and every leash and verbal correction must be
considered an integral part of every correction given. Praise
cannot be emphasized enough. Such phrases as, "That's a
good boy," "Good boy," "Atta boy," are important in order
to reassure the dog. It tells him that you are not angry with

him and that love and approval are always there, providing
he obeys properly. Once you correct the dog you must
always praise him whether he performs properly or not.
He must never associate any correction with punishment.
It is simply a line of communication that tells him he was
incorrect.

For most dogs you must jerk the leash firmly in order to
get an effective correction. This requires the use of both
hands holding the leash and jerking it to the side with
only the amount of force necessary to create a sensation
around the animal's neck. It should never be pulled hard
enough to yank the dog off his legs or give him any pain
whatsoever.

Common sense will tell you which dogs must be corrected in a gentle manner. Extremely aggressive dogs, shy
dogs, nervous dogs, frail and fragile dogs, and most puppies
require a gentle leash correction. However, the typical adult
dog can be corrected with a firm jerk of the leash.

*Never correct your dog while you are teaching him the
basics of a command. However, once he has demonstrated
that he has learned the command it is fair to correct him
if he refuses to obey or makes a mistake.*

To review the leash correction: Snap the leash quickly
and firmly upward and to the right when he refuses to obey
or makes a mistake. As you do this say, "NO," in a firm
tone of voice. Release the tension on the leash instantly
and then praise the dog lovingly. That is a proper leash
correction.

Vocal Control and Body Language

Vocal Control. Two important training tools are your
voice and your body. When giving your dog a verbal com-

mand or correction, a firm, resonant sound must come out of your mouth. When delivering a command your voice must be calm, firm, and authoritative in a friendly way. When correcting the dog with the word "NO" the voice must sound different. Shouting is no good. Draw in a deep breath of air and allow it to expand the muscles of the stomach. As you allow the air to escape say the word "NO" so that it rides out with the released breath. You will immediately notice a deeper, firmer tone of voice than you have ever produced and it will not reflect any unnecessary harshness or emotional overtones. This is the proper way to say "NO" and expect to command the dog's attention.

When it is time to give your canine student his due praise for obeying a command properly it should be done in a high-pitched tone of voice that reflects your happiness and approval. Because dogs are like babies that never grow up they may be spoken to in that manner. They love it.

Body Language. Body language, as the term implies, pertains to what you communicate to your dog with the way you stand, walk and move. Do not expect your dog to accept you as a dominant figure if your body language indicates uncertainty, indecisiveness, and, worst of all, submissiveness. It's like shaking hands with someone whose fingers feel like a loose washcloth around your hand. A limp handshake does not communicate sincerity. Rather, it communicates insecurity and other negative possibilities.

You must stand straight and tall when training your dog. Move with a sense of precision and determination. The best professional dog trainers look something like dancers with sharp, quick turns when they work their dogs. If you feel confident your body language will communicate confidence to the dog and get him to pay attention to you. Dogs will not learn much from a person that moves like a subordinate member of his pack. Leadership, as expressed through your body language, springs from an inner feeling about yourself. If you do not feel like your dog's pack leader, then you must pretend that you do. Do not become confused about who is at which end of the leash. If you conduct yourself with the firm-but-gentle manner of a determined parent, you won't go wrong.

On the other hand, totally dominating a shy, nervous or very small dog with your body language is counterproductive. Never pull a dog too hard or too sharply so that he is yanked off his feet. That is too much body language. If your dog is as small as a toy breed and you tower over him by standing too close he will be totally intimidated. The objective is to create a dominant or leader-of-the-pack perception of you and yet still maintain a happy, loving relationship with your dog. You must not cause the dog to fear you or dread his obedience training sessions.

If your dog is small, stand a little farther away from him than you would if he were bigger. You must give your small dog an opportunity to see you without looking up as if you were a fifty-story office building. You might even kneel to him during the breaks and get down to a level where he can relate to you. The same applies to insecure, frightened, or shy dogs. Your dog's personality should determine your body language.

"NO" and "OKAY"

These are two verbal tools that are not only invaluable for dog training, they are absolutely essential.

"NO" means your dog must stop whatever he is doing

when this verbal command is given. "NO" is most commonly used as a correction and is never said during the teaching process. A dog can never be corrected for something he has not been taught.

Although negative words and tones of voice are not fun they are a blessing when they are concisely used in a crisp, clear manner. The average dog cannot understand sentences such as "Get out of there," "Get your head out of the garbage," "Get off the bed," etc. It is also impossible to get a dog to stop what he's doing if you give him a command such as "SIT," or "DOWN." The dog cannot stop one action and begin another simply because you have commanded him to do so. He must be stopped from his first action and then commanded to start another. "NO" will accomplish that.

All dogs respond to the human voice according to its tone. If you say "NO" in a very mild tone of voice it is not really clear to the animal that he is supposed to stop what he is doing. If you exert too much force or emotion (anger, frustration, rage), the dog will be too frightened or confused to do anything but cower, attack, urinate, or do any combination of the three. You must learn to snap out "NO" in a loud, firm tone of voice that startles the dog into stopping his action but does not make him scared to death of you.

When correcting your dog with the word "NO" the voice must sound different. Shouting is no good. Draw in a deep breath of air and allow it to expand the muscles of the stomach. As you allow the air to escape say the word "NO" so that it rides out with the released breath. This will give you a deeper, firmer tone of voice and will communicate a clear meaning to your dog. "NO" means stop.

"OKAY" means one of two things. First, it is a release

from training or walking in HEEL. It is also used as a prefix to the dog's name when utilizing the command RECALL. Just as your dog must know when a command is being given he must also be able to distinguish when the discipline is over. The verbal tool "OKAY" must be positive in sound and represent something very pleasant to the dog. If it does not it is absolutely useless. If the word is said with irritation or any tone other than an exuberant one it will defeat its purpose. It is also important that you do not confuse the dog by using the word for any but its expressed purpose.

After a training session the dog should be told that the learning is over for the day and told in as pleasant a tone as possible. "OKAY" can be said in a high-pitched voice or simply in a cheerful, happy tone. The higher you pitch your voice (as if talking to a baby) the more excited and happy the dog will be. "*Okay*, Maggie; that's all," should make your dog feel deliriously happy and bring a jumping, running response.

When walking in the HEEL position the dog is on the owner's left side with her head near the trainer's left thigh. There is approximately two feet of leash extended from the owner's hand to the dog's collar. The limited length of leash greatly restricts the dog's freedom as both walk down the street. It is not until the animal reaches the area where she usually eliminates that she is released from the restricted length of the leash. This release is accomplished with the verbal tool "OKAY." Assuming you are walking on the sidewalk you say "OKAY" in a very happy tone of voice and allow the dog to have all the leash she needs or wants (never release the leash entirely). This release will become extremely important to the dog and she will look to you in anticipation, waiting for permission to eliminate at the correct location.

One is never one hundred percent sure that the dog will come when she is called if she is off-leash and outdoors. This requires long and arduous training and is very difficult for dogs one year or older to learn. If the dog does not associate the use of her name with something pleasant (your praise) she may not come to you. It is here that "OKAY" becomes very valuable. When the dog is some distance away you must raise your voice to be heard by her. To counter that effect you should call the dog by prefixing her name with "OKAY," and use a very exuberant sound. It should be, "*Okay*, Maggie, come!" If you say it properly, the dog will be reassured that you are not calling her in order to punish her. "OKAY" is one of the more positive sounding words in the language and is very difficult to say in anything but a cheerful tone of voice.

The Command *SIT*

The dog will assume a sitting posture on command. The dog's body is upright with his front paws standing straight as his rear weight rests on his haunches.

Holding the Leash. Teaching SIT requires two pieces of equipment: the training collar and the six-foot leather leash. Place the dog by your left side as you both face the same forward direction. The dog, it is assumed, is standing on all fours. The leash loosely dangles across your knees and up to your right hand. The thumb of the right hand is inserted into the very top of the loop while the rest of the hand clasps entirely around the loop. Next, gather all but two feet of the leash and include it in your grip. The gathered four feet of the leash hangs down on your right leg in the form of one large loop. You are now in a position of maximum control over the dog.

Teaching SIT. The next step after placing yourself and the dog in the proper position (and holding the leash correctly) is giving the vocal command. With a firm voice say, "SIT," and then gently push the dog's hindquarters down with your left hand. Keep pushing slowly until she has no choice but to be in a sitting position. Do not push too hard or too fast. Once the dog has reached the sitting position give her lavish praise even though she did not get there on her own. It is the only way she knows what you expect of her. The praise is her reward for obeying your command. Be patient. When praising the dog do not pet her or make any body contact.

This command is easy to teach. You simply repeat the above fifteen or twenty times. By then the dog should be going into a SIT position without your pushing her into it. Your vocal command "SIT" will suffice. Do not correct the dog for any reason during this teaching process. Introducing a negative note while teaching something new will only make the dog have a negative association with the new command. This is important.

Correcting the dog is allowed once she has learned the command. After being taught SIT or any other command the dog will, from time to time, refuse to obey your order. It is then appropriate to administer a leash correction accompanied by a firm, "NO." Give her immediate praise after the dog responds to the correction.

The first teaching session requires that you repeat the command twenty times. After that, allow the dog a short rest and then repeat the command another twenty times. During the rest period do not allow the animal to decide that the lesson is over for the day. That is accomplished by avoiding any play or extensive walks. By the second half of the training session the dog should have learned SIT by vocal command only. If not, one more entire session will be necessary but not without one hour rest.

You may now end the training session. Always end the session on a note of success when the dog has accomplished his task well. End the session in a definite manner. Say to the dog, "OKAY," and then walk away from the training area in a definite manner. Your dog may want a walk or he may be tired and simply desire to go home and take a nap. Repeat this procedure every day for six days. Practice sessions are important before moving on to the next command.

The Command *HEEL*

The dog must walk when given the command and carefully pace herself so that she never pulls ahead or lags behind. She is on the left side of her owner with her head approximately next to the left knee.

In no command is the proper position of the leash more important than in HEEL. With two feet of leash draped across the front of your knees, hold it firmly in the right hand, which must always be comfortably situated next to your right thigh. Holding the leash for HEEL is exactly as described earlier in "The Leash Correction" (See page 117). During the teaching of this command it will be necessary to use both hands to hold the leash so that firm jerks can be implemented.

This teaching process begins with the dog in SIT. You and the dog should be side by side, facing in the same direction. Hold the leash in your right hand, allowing enough slack so that it drapes across the knees. Because HEEL is an action command, you must use the dog's name before saying the command word itself. Using the dog's name alerts her to forward motion and allows her the slight pause necessary to respond properly. Saying the dog's name also get her attention so she will focus on you, ready to move forward. The full command should be, "MAGGIE, [pause] HEEL." Then walk forward, starting out with the *left* foot. This is important because the dog sees your left foot first. When it moves so will she. You will then be starting out together and that is the beginning of the correct way to walk in HEEL.

At first the dog will run ahead because that is what she has probably always done. Allow her to run ahead, using up the full length of the six-foot leash. Make a fast right turn when she gets to the end of it. The dog will be pulled hard and it will surprise her. At the instant of maximum stress repeat the vocal command "MAGGIE, HEEL." Without a pause quickly walk in the opposite direction, being sure that the leash is on your left side. The dog will have no choice but to turn and walk in your direction as she stumbles along to catch up. When she does, give her lavish praise. This will require a firm assertion of your will over the dog's.

Do not stop or slow down. The dog will overcome her confusion and eventually catch up with you. Praise her and readjust the leash to the length with which you started. Most certainly the dog will run ahead again. Repeat the technique with absolutely no regard for her discomfort. Continue walking and making right turns. Maintain a steady walking rhythm until the dog catches up. When she does, adjust the length of the leash to the normal two feet across your knees. One cannot emphasize enough the importance of the praise each time the dog catches up. The constant turning procedure is hard on her psyche and she is not sure if you are angry with her. The praise helps to guide her. She will soon associate walking by your side with your approval.

Some dogs tend to lag behind. This may start after two

or three heeling lessons when the dog has stopped darting forward. Playfully encourage the animal to walk with you, to catch up, to keep pace. If the sound of your voice is enthusiastic and friendly the dog will bound to you and then keep her attention upward on your face. Pat your left thigh with your hand to get her attention.

The exact position for HEEL is by your left side; the dog's head is approximately next to your left knee. After several lessons it becomes important to maintain exactitude. In the early lessons the dog will have done all right if she only stayed two or three feet ahead. It is now time that she be corrected whenever she strays away from the correct place.

Whenever the dog fails to maintain the exact, correct position, do the following: Jerk the leash firmly, say, "MAGGIE, HEEL!," execute a right turn, and walk in the opposite direction. Give the dog immediate praise. The praise keeps the dog informed that you are not angry and that she is now doing the correct thing. Do this again and again and again throughout each lesson until the dog is heeling in the true sense of the command.

Conduct two fifteen minute sessions a day, four hours apart. Practice walking in HEEL as often as possible. Take long walks every day and utilize the teaching procedures each time. Practice makes perfect. After the initial teaching session, repeat the procedures for six days, along with the preceding lessons, before teaching a new command.

Do not teach HEEL to a young puppy or you risk impairing her pleasant personality. A puppy should be allowed her natural curiosity and instinct to run ahead, to the full extent of her leash.

Select an enclosed area that is distraction-free with sufficient room to walk back and forth. Put the dog through the paces of all that she has been previously taught. Praise the dog lavishly for performing well.

Gauge the strength of the leash correction to the size, temperament, and age of your dog. Do not overdo it in any case.

After fifteen minutes end the lesson by saying "OKAY," and then walk the dog home for a rest.

In the second fifteen minute session return to the training area with the dog. The next lesson involves teaching your dog to go into a SIT position whenever you come to a full stop.

The Command *HEEL-SIT*

When walking in HEEL the dog will respond to a stop by going into the SIT position. The dog stops every time the trainer does and sits without being commanded to do so.

This is accomplished by alerting the dog that a stop is coming up. The signal for stopping is simply a reduction of your walking speed. If the dog is focused on you she will be sensitive to any change of pace. As you slow down, so will she.

During the teaching process give the dog the command "SIT" every time you stop. As you verbally give the command raise the leash tautly above his head twelve inches. Assuming he has already learned the command SIT this is all that is necessary. Repeat this procedure many times until she sits without the verbal command. Never use the dog's name when giving this command. SIT is not an action command and you do not want any forward motion when giving it. Every time the dog sits on command give her well-deserved praised.

If your dog does not HEEL-SIT after she has been taught

to do so, you may execute a leash correction and give a firm "NO!" It is not fair to correct a dog before she has been taught what to do. But after one or two lessons it can be assumed that she knows what to do and is simply testing your authority or is disinterested or is forgetful. In any case the leash correction and the sharp "NO!" remind her what to do. Praise the dog immediately after she has obeyed the command, even though she had to be corrected.

Occasionally a dog will not even respond properly to the leash correction when commanded to SIT from the HEEL position. Repeat the leash correction and give her the command "SIT." Pull the leash twelve inches above the dog's head and push her haunches down into a sitting position with your left hand. This technique must be used only as a last resort. It is not a good idea, usually, to give a command following a leash correction. It can create a bad association for the dog. She must always anticipate praise with every command given rather than correction.

It should not take too many corrections and repetitions for the dog to execute the HEEL-SIT properly and without benefit of verbal commands. You will be pleased to walk down a street with your dog in perfect HEEL and have her stop and sit as you wait for the traffic light to change or if you decide to stop and talk to someone.

End every lesson on a high note of praise so that the dog will anticipate her next with pleasure. The way to do this is to finish each session when the animal obeys the new command correctly for the first time. Convey to her your exuberant pleasure and allow her to relieve herself.

The Command STAY
(SIT-STAY or DOWN-STAY)

*After being given the proper verbal command and hand
signal the dog must hold her SIT or DOWN position until
she is released by her owner. She should look straight ahead
and move very little.*

The command STAY is used in connection with the command SIT and the command DOWN depending on what
you require at the moment. SIT-STAY is useful for a short
STAY period, when the dog must wait for you to finish
talking to someone. DOWN-STAY is important when your
dog is placed in a corner of a room as you entertain guests
in your home. The only difference in teaching one from the
other is how you place the dog during the teaching process.

Teaching STAY requires the use of three techniques. The
first is a verbal command. The second is a hand signal.
The third is a pivotal turning motion on the ball of your
left foot.

Verbal Command. With the dog on your left side both
you and the animal are facing in the same direction. Give
her the command "SIT." Praise her after she goes into the
proper position. Next, give her the command "STAY." The
hand signal accompanies the verbal command.

Hand Signal. Hold the leash with your right hand and
allow enough to drape across your knees so there is a little
slack plus the width of your body. The signal is given with
the left hand. Flatten your left hand and keep all fingers
straight and close together as if you were going to use it
for swimming. As you give the command "STAY," place
your left hand in front of the dog's eyes leaving about

four inches of space so that you don't touch him. The hand signal is accomplished quickly and merely blocks the dog's vision for a second. Return your left hand to your side one or two seconds after blocking the dog's vision. Eventually, the dog will remain in the STAY with the use of the hand signal exclusively.

Pivotal Turning Motion. The objective is to make a pivotal turn so that you will face the dog without stirring her as you effect the turn. To accomplish this you use the left foot as a pivot and do not move it from its original position. Step off with your right foot and turn to face the animal. Allow your left foot to revolve in place as your right foot moves forward one step so that you are almost facing the dog. After you have placed the right foot on the ground, facing the dog, move the left foot next to it so that you have accomplished the complete turn and are now facing the dog. If you do this any other than the prescribed way, the dog will assume you are about to say HEEL and start moving.

Teaching STAY

Start out teaching STAY with the dog in the SIT position. After you are satisfied that she knows the command, then teach it all over again in the DOWN position (see The Command DOWN, page 135). While doing the pivotal turn maintain the leash eighteen inches straight above the dog's head. The leash should be taut so that the animal cannot move as you turn to face her. It is not productive to keep the leash too tight because that might frighten the dog and make her want to run away. It is this firm leash control that forces the dog to associate remaining in position with the verbal command, "STAY."

From the beginning of the verbal command "STAY," to the hand signal and the pivotal turn, only a few seconds should have gone by. This should be repeated fifteen times. Always praise the dog after successfully completing each and every turn despite the fact that she had to be held in place with the taut leash. Part of the teaching process is standing in front of the dog for a full twenty seconds after effecting each turn. The idea of remaining in STAY will be absorbed by the dog and a conditioned reflex to the command will begin to develop. The pivotal turn is merely a teaching tool and will not be used after the dog has learned the command properly.

Back Away. Back away as the dog remains in STAY. Give the verbal command "STAY," accompany it with the hand signal, make a turn so that you are facing the dog. Maintain the eighteen inches of leash tautly above the dog's head with the right hand. Once you are standing in front of the dog, place the leash in your left hand and grasp the leash as in the leash correction. The right hand then grasps only the main line of the leash, directly under the left hand, and holds it loosely. As you back away, the leash should be able to slide freely through the right hand allowing it to extend. This prevents any slack from developing as you back away. This is important so that you will be able to correct the dog if she tries to move out of position as you back away.

You should now back away from the dog. The leash slides through your right hand as it is held firmly by the left and gets longer as you move backward. The dog may begin to walk toward you as you move away. If she does, give her the verbal command "STAY" and move in toward her. Pull the leash through your right hand as you move forward and hold it once again eighteen inches above her head. The leash must always be taut so as to force the dog to remain in the SIT position. Always pull the leash slightly to the side as you move in so you avoid hitting the dog with the metal clip. Stepping toward the dog will stop her from moving. Once the dog has stopped moving she must be praised. Pause for several seconds and then begin backing away again. Keep moving until the dog tries to move. You may get back a little farther this time. Repeat the procedure. Step in toward the dog as you pull the leash through your right hand, keeping it taut and above the dog's head. Praise her for stopping and wait several seconds before moving away. Continue this technique until you can back away a full six feet (the full length of the leash) while the dog sits in STAY. Once the dog will STAY for the entire length of the leash, repeat the process fifteen times.

Half Way Around. Repeat everything you've done to this point, but this time try walking half way around the dog's right side. Once she allows you to do that without leaving her position, try walking around her left side. If she leaves her STAY position say "NO" in a firm tone of voice and start over. Repeat each new phase fifteen times.

Walking Completely Around. Repeat everything you've done to this point, but this time walk all the way around the dog, making a complete circle. In all probability, he will turn his head in order to follow you with his eyes. This is perfectly acceptable providing he does not leave his STAY position. Repeat the circling action ten times, as you repeat the command "STAY," in a soothing tone of voice. Praise the dog after completing each circle but do not praise the dog too enthusiastically or he will think the training session is over.

Once you are satisfied he has learned the command STAY release him from the session, saying in an enthusiastic tone of voice, "OKAY," and then walk him home. Always end each session on a positive, upbeat note. The dog will be tired so he should be allowed to sleep. Repeat these procedures every day for six days.

The Command *DOWN*

On command the dog lowers his entire body to the ground or the floor. Although he is completely relaxed, his head remains erect as he looks forward in anticipation of your next command. The dog's front paws are stretched out in front of him forming two parallel straight lines. His rear paws are holding his resting body weight.

This is the most difficult of all commands to teach a dog. Going into a DOWN position is the ultimate submission for a dog. Not only does he feel vulnerable to attack but it is the most complete acceptance of the trainer's dominance. If your dog is one year old or more, if he is a very stubborn, very nervous, or very aggressive animal, then it may be best to skip this command and let a professional dog trainer teach it. The dog may balk and become uncooperative. If you are gentle but firm, if the dog is young and has been properly obedient throughout the training and if the dog is of even temperament, then proceed to teach this command yourself.

Teach the dog this command on a smooth surface, such as a linoleum or hardwood floor. It is easier to get the dog into the correct DOWN position even if he is unwilling at first.

A word about the vocal intonation of the voice command "DOWN." When saying the command, extend the middle sound of the word so that it comes out in an exaggerated manner. "DOWWWWnnnn." It somehow helps the dog do what you want. The trailing sound of the word suggests to him what is expected.

There are two effective techniques to teach DOWN and the one chosen must be determined by the nature of the dog involved. The techniques are 1) pulling the dog by the front paws into a DOWN position as you give the command or 2) pushing the dog into a DOWN position by applying pressure to the leash with the bottom of your foot.

The most direct and uncomplicated technique is the first, pulling the dog's paws forward. However, a large dog may be too difficult to maneuver in this manner. An aggressive dog may bite when pulled at the paws. Technique Number Two, applying pressure to the leash with the foot to lower the dog to the ground on command, is the most practical one for training a large or uncooperative dog. It is also the safest method.

Teaching DOWN

Technique Number One. Place the dog in the SIT-STAY position. Stand beside him as in HEEL. Hold the leash with the right hand. Leave a small amount of slack so it drapes. Pivot with the left foot and place the right foot in front of the dog. Bring both feet together once you are facing the dog. The leash should be held above the dog's head to keep him in position. Kneel to the ground and take hold of both front paws with one hand if you can. Say the command, "DOWWWWnnnn," and gently but firmly pull the front paws forward. For puppies, small dogs, and even-tempered dogs there is no choice but to slide into the DOWN position. Once the dog is in the DOWN position, heap lavish praise on him. Next, give him the commands

"SIT," and "STAY." Once again, praise the dog. Repeat this teaching procedure at least fifteen times and give the dog a ten-minute break. Allow him to relieve himself. After the break repeat the procedure until the dog offers no resistance whatsoever to being pulled into the DOWN position. You are now ready to teach the hand signal for DOWN unless you cannot succeed with Technique Number One and must try Technique Number Two.

Technique Number Two. (If you have used Technique Number One successfully, skip this section and go directly to The Hand Signal.) This is an alternative to the first technique if the dog is large, stubborn or aggressive. Place the dog in the SIT-STAY position. Stand beside the dog as in HEEL. Hold the leash with both hands. Allow a little more slack than usual so it drapes closer to the ground. Raise the left foot and place it on top of the leash at the center of the drape. Say, "DOWWWWWnnnn." As the voice descends in tone, press the leash down with the left foot. This will force the dog to go down. Even a large, stubborn dog will slide down if the floor is somewhat slippery. As you push down with the foot, you must slide the leash upward across the bottom of the shoe. Do not pull up on the leash too quickly or too harshly. As the dog descends, pull the leash upward in a slow but steady manner. When the dog reaches the ground, praise him enthusiastically. Allow him to remain in the DOWN position for ten seconds and then say, "SIT." Praise him and then say, "STAY," using the proper STAY hand signal as previously taught. Praise him again. Repeat this procedure fifteen times and give the dog a ten-minute break. Allow him to relieve himself. After the break repeat the procedure until the dog offers no resistance to going into the DOWN position. You are now ready to teach the hand signal for DOWN.

The Hand Signal. Whether you used Technique One or Two to maneuver the dog into the DOWN position, you must now add the use of your hand as part of the command. Place the dog in SIT-STAY position. Kneel next to the dog at his right side facing in the same direction as the dog. Hold the leash with the right hand across your chest and keep it taut. With a tight leash he can do nothing but SIT. Flatten your left hand as if for a military salute. Raise the left arm above the dog's head. Say the command, "DOWWWWWnnnn," and lower the left arm so that the dog can see it coming down, past his eyes and onto the top of the taut leash at the clip. By now the dog should be lowering his body in response to the voice command. While you are still saying "DOWWWWWnnnn," your left hand should be pressing the leash all the way to the ground. Once the dog is in the DOWN position praise him lavishly and then say, "SIT" and then say, "STAY." Repeat this entire procedure fifteen times. The objective is to associate your lowering hand with the command DOWN in the mind of your trained dog. Once this is accomplished you will be able to stand a good distance from the dog and simply give him the hand signal to which he will respond as he should. This could save his life in an outdoor traffic situation. If the dog does not respond properly or resists the teaching of this part of the lesson, place him in SIT-STAY position and begin again.

Once the dog is accustomed to seeing the hand come down onto the leash from the side, it is important to acclimate him to the hand coming down from the front. Place him in SIT-STAY with the dog at your left side, as in HEEL. Pivot around so that you are standing in front of the dog. This time hold the leash with the left hand, keeping it taut, as before. Kneel on one knee, flatten the right hand, raise the right arm above your head, keeping it straight, and then say the command "DOWWWWWnnnn." As you say the command, you must lower your arm, in full sight of the dog, landing on top of the leash, palm facing down. You may or may not have to apply pressure to the leash to force the dog into the DOWN position. At this time the dog should be moving into position at the sound of the command. Praise him for obeying you. Place him in SIT and STAY. Repeat all this fifteen times or until the dog obeys both voice command and hand signal. Do not tolerate playfulness or any other avoidance behavior. When this happens, start over from the SIT-STAY position.

Obeying the Command Without Pressure on the Leash. If the dog is not yet exhausted, take him through this one last step. The objective is to teach him to respond to the voice command and the hand signal for DOWN without the trainer kneeling or applying pressure of any kind to the leash.

Stand in front of the dog from a distance of two feet. Allow as much slack in the leash as possible and hold it with the left hand. Give the command "SIT," praise the dog for obeying. Give the command "STAY," using the proper hand signal, and praise the dog for obeying. If the dog does not obey these commands, deliver a leash correction while saying "NO." If the results are still not satisfactory, start over at the dog's side. Repeat this procedure after making a pivotal turn to face the dog, as you have been doing throughout the training course.

Assuming the dog has obeyed properly, you are ready to continue. He should be in a SIT-STAY position while you are standing in front of him. Flatten your right hand as if for a salute. Raise your right arm above your head in a straight line. Say the command "DOWWWWWnnnn," and lower the right arm onto the leash at the same time. The dog will probably obey the command and go down without any pressure from the right hand. Praise him and start over again without moving from the frontal position. Give him the SIT and STAY commands and then the DOWN command, repeating the above procedures fifteen times. Do not forget the very important hand signals.

You may try repeating this procedure from greater distances. At first, give the commands from the end of the fully extended leash. If the dog continues to respond properly, try it from six feet away without holding onto the leash at all. Be ready to step in quickly to grab the leash and deliver a leash correction if the dog moves or bolts from the proper position. If you are still experiencing success, try the command from two, three or even six feet away from the dropped leash. Always be prepared to make a quick grab for the leash if the dog bolts. End the session by saying "OKAY," in a happy, enthusiastic tone of voice and then walk home.

Practice. Practice. Practice. Conduct one twenty-minute practice session every day for six days. Review everything the dog has been taught up until this point in each practice session.

The Command *RECALL*

The owner uses a precise verbal command and a hand signal so that the dog stops what he is doing, runs to the one who has called him, and places himself in a SIT position when he reaches his destination. Some trainers refer to this command as "Come When Called."

The RECALL is an extremely valuable command, one that could someday save the dog's life in traffic. It is extremely valuable to be able to command your dog to return to you after he has darted away for something that has captured his interest.

The verbal command is extremely important to the successful teaching and execution of this command. Your voice must communicate to the dog that something wonderful is happening. Because this command involves forward motion, the dog's name is always said just before the word *come*. To further convey an exciting feeling, we use the word *okay* in front of the dog's name. The command, therefore, is "OKAY, MURRAY, COME," with the stress on the word OKAY. If you always use the command in this manner, the dog will never be confused and will want to obey.

Never correct the dog while teaching this command. Never correct the dog after he has obeyed this command. When the dog comes on command he should receive nothing but the highest praise, so that he will always obey the command with enthusiasm. No dog will run to a human if he has experienced something unpleasant for his trouble.

Teaching THE RECALL

At the start of the lesson repeat everything the dog has learned up to this point. Then, place the dog in SIT-STAY. With the leash in the left hand, stand in front of the dog, facing him, five feet away. Allow a slight slack in the leash.

Call the dog with the proper command, "OKAY, MURRAY, COME," in an extremely exuberant tone of voice. Because of your enthusiasm, the dog should move forward and come when called. If he does, give him heaps of praise for it. Return the dog to his original position and once again place him in SIT and STAY. Repeat the procedure fifteen times. If he does not come, then add more excitement to the tone of your voice. Almost any dog will respond. *Do not correct your dog for not coming to you.*

Once again place the dog in SIT-STAY. Stand in front of the dog, facing him, five feet away, with the leash in the left hand. Give the command, "OKAY, MURRAY, COME," while gently snapping the leash forward. The gentle snap of the leash should be on the word OKAY. When the dog moves to your feet, give him lots of praise. He should be thrilled and delighted about obeying this command. Return him to the original position and place him once again in SIT-STAY. Repeat the procedure fifteen times and take a break.

The Hand Signal. This gesture is quite simple. One raises the right arm from the side and swings it around and across the chest. It is the same gesture one might make to call someone from afar.

Place the dog in SIT-STAY. Stand in front of the dog, facing him five feet away, with the leash in the left hand. Give the command, "OKAY, MURRAY, COME," as you gently snap the leash forward, *and then give the hand signal.* Remember, the leash is snapped on the word OKAY. The dog should be praised deliriously when he gets to your feet. Return him to his original position and place him in SIT-STAY. Repeat this step fifteen times. Rest a few minutes and then repeat it fifteen times again.

SIT ON RECALL. It is now time to teach the last phase of this command, and that is the SIT ON RECALL. Place the dog in SIT-STAY. Stand in front of the dog, facing him, five feet away with the leash in the left hand. Give the command, "OKAY, MURRAY, COME," gently snapping the leash on the word OKAY. Immediately after giving the hand signal, but as the arm moves forward, grab the leash and begin to pull it in, first with one arm and then the other so that it is held above the dog's head tautly when he gets to your feet. The dog must have no choice but to SIT once he is directly in front of you. Then give the command, "SIT," praise the dog lavishly, and then give the command, "STAY," accompanied by the proper hand signal for STAY, and once again praise the dog. Return him to his original position, and place him in SIT-STAY. Repeat the entire procedure fifteen times.

End the teaching session by saying, "OKAY," in a happy tone of voice and by walking home. Conduct one twenty-minute practice session every day for six days. Always review everything the dog has been taught in each session.

You may now consider your dog obedience trained. But there is always more that a dog (and his owner) can learn. There are training classes you can attend; private training sessions available from professionals; and clubs to join that are involved with Obedience Trials competition sponsored by the American Kennel Club, the United Kennel Club, and various other competitions. Continuing your dog's training and then using it in competition can be a very enjoyable and worthwhile activity.

6

HOUSE-TRAINING
YOUR DOG

Of all dog behavioral problems, this is the one that is the most troubling for pet owners. If a dog can be house-trained early, he is assured of keeping his home and enjoying a full life of comfort and happiness. Dogs cannot understand the human revulsion caused by body waste. In the natural setting, a dog's body waste is important to him because of its various uses. It is a dynamic example of important canine behavior conflicting with human needs and, to some extent, obsessions. More than a few dogs have lost their homes because of their failure to adjust their behavior accordingly. House-training is therefore of vital importance to all concerned, but especially to the dog.

A fully grown dog's house-training problems are simply a matter of good training techniques, assuming that the dog is not sick. But the novice dog owner must understand that this is not the case for a puppy. A puppy has a very small stomach and an even smaller bladder, not to mention undeveloped sphincter muscle control, and needs a great deal of help to become house-trained. Puppy owners must be patient and sympathetic with a young dog's limitations when attempting to train him from urinating and defecating all over the floor of their home.

House-training becomes somewhat more bearable and

easier to accomplish when the dog owner understands the nature of canine elimination, how it works, and what it means to a dog.

For the first three weeks in a puppy's life, his brain is confined to performing only the most fundamental tasks, such as seeking mother's warmth and milk. There is little mental activity. During this period, the process of urination and defecation is accomplished by a reflex promoted by the mother's licking of the puppy's stomach, genitals, and anus. This stimulation begins the involuntary act of elimination. It is her instinct to keep the nest clean and to accomplish this she ingests the puppies' waste. One can only speculate about a dog's instinct to maintain a clean nest.

On the twenty-first day of life (the end of the third week), the puppy's brain develops further. Its organs begin to function independently, allowing sight, smell, hearing, taste, and independent elimination. At this stage the puppy can crawl out of its nest, eliminate, and then return. At first the puppy leaves the nest to eliminate wherever he is capable of going. By the eighth week the puppy is no longer crawling and walks deliberately to specific locations outside the nest in order to eliminate. It has been indelibly imprinted in his brain by the example set by his mother not to eliminate in his own nest. The puppy will wait many hours during the night and soil the nest only out of desperation if he is prevented from leaving it. During the day the puppy exercises less control and eliminates more frequently. Until the little dog is twelve weeks old, he is going to eliminate at least every hour or two, as long as he is awake.

There are two important behavioral patterns in all puppies that help dog owners immeasurably when trying to house-train their pets. First, no puppy wants to dirty his own nest and will try not to when confined there. Also, he needs space to circle around in when he's about to eliminate. Most puppies turn quickly and make circular movements before letting go. When confined to the small area of the nest, it becomes difficult to turn around in circles.

Second, all dogs eight weeks and older look for their own scent or that of another dog on top of which to urinate or defecate. This is *scent posting* behavior. Once a puppy (or an older dog) has established several toilet locations, he is always drawn back to them, unless they have been deodorized and voided of his scent. This is extremely useful information for house-training because it enables the dog owner to allow the scent to remain in a desirable place or eliminate it in a less desirable place. The dog owner can actually select where the dog will eliminate his body waste by allowing the scent to remain there.

Researchers believe that scent posting has to do with marking off a territory that belongs to the dog. When one dog urinates on top of another dog's urine spot, he is imposing his presence and sense of superiority on the other dog. This represents a subtle form of infighting without actual combat. It is interesting that in a wolf pack only the leader lifts his leg and marks off territory. Our dogs may accept us as the leader of the pack, but they take the full responsibility of marking territory because we seem to be remiss in performing that important function. From the dog's point of view, no pack is properly established without claiming territory by scent posting. Marking the area with urine has also to do with mating, declarations of one's presence in the area, and pack domination.

A female dog's elimination is somewhat different from that of the male. Female dogs are also attracted to scent posts, but do not wander too far from home. Like puppies of both genders, female dogs squat to eliminate. Females experience two periods of estrus (or heat) a year and will wander a little farther from home at that time. During estrus the female scent posts with her urine, which has a special odor to it. A male dog becomes intensely interested and sexually aroused when sniffing the urine mark of a female in heat. Here, the point to scent posting is for the purpose of mating.

The Important Methods of House-Training

With the exception of the "rub-their-noses-in-it" method, most house-training techniques are effective. But there isn't a technique available that doesn't demand of the owner a great deal of time, patience, and energy. Beware of those that try to convince you that a harsh, physically abusive manner is the best way to house-train a dog. Harsh methods are inhumane and destructive to both human and canine. It is important to understand that you can never successfully house-train your dog by hitting or hollering. It just doesn't work. If you attempted to toilet-train a baby that way, you would only succeed in creating psychological damage that would take a lifetime to fix. The same applies to dogs.

When you hit a dog because the dog soiled the house, you are punishing the animal for obeying his most natural and necessary instinctive behavior. Remember, besides ridding the body of waste material, dogs urinate and defecate for the purpose of claiming territory, asserting pack leadership, mating, etc. To physically punish him for doing what he was born to do creates unnatural behavior and demands that the dog behave unlike a dog. *The key to house-training is to redirect your dog's behavior, rather than to change it or eliminate it.*

You can house-train a dog with one of several effective methods. If you live in the country, or have a backyard in the city or suburbs, you may simply open the door and let the dog go out to do his business. Of course, you will never be able to trust your dog indoors to control himself if that is how you approach the subject.

The only practical options for house-training are *housebreaking* and *paper-training*. However, these two training techniques confuse most dog owners who may not even realize that they are quite different from one another. A clear, concise definition of each technique is essential.

Housebreaking

Housebreaking is a technique for conditioning a dog to relieve himself outdoors only, when being walked or allowed out.

A Five-Point Housebreaking Method

1. **Correcting the Dog.** Among the many misconceptions of dog training, hitting the dog is the greatest. It is a mistake to think that the dog has learned something by being hit or yelled at or by having his nose rubbed in his own mess. The underlying philosophy of this method of housebreaking is simply that the word *correction* must be substituted for the word *punishment*.

You can correct the dog only when you witness the mistake. The mental grasp of most dogs is extremely limited. Therefore, a dog cannot associate a smack on the rump with a mess on the floor he made before you arrived on the scene. Even a few short minutes after he messes is enough time to make him stare dumbfoundedly and wonder why you are hollering. Punishment, even proper correction, effects very little after the fact.

How to correct your dog. Assuming the dog is urinating or defecating indoors during the housebreaking period, and is doing it in front of you, there is only one way to respond. You must startle the dog so that he stops what he is doing and then run him outside to finish.

Do not holler, hit, or threaten the animal. Do not use rolled-up newspaper or a pointed, accusing finger to terrorize him. Create a noisemaker out of an empty soda can by placing five or more pennies inside and taping it closed. It is here that the noisemaker comes into play.

Here is the proper sequence for correcting your dog: The dog transgresses. You shake the noisemaker vigorously, making a loud racket and accompany the noise with a firm "NO!" The dog will be startled and look up at you. Moving quickly, place his leash and collar on and run him outside to finish what he started. Once he does, praise him lavishly. The result is that you have stopped the dog from messing completely on the floor while *teaching* him where that process is to take place. *This is the only effective way the dog can be taught.*

Use your common sense in how vigorously you shake the noisemaking can. Do not win the battle of housebreaking while losing the war of obedience training. A shy or nervous dog can become acutely disturbed by too intense a correction and may become aggressive as a result. Adjust the intensity of the correction to the temperament of your dog. The tone of your voice when saying "NO" must also be modulated in this situation.

The most important aspect of the correction is the verbal part of the correction, "NO." This must always be said when the can is shaken so that the dog will eventually respond to the word itself without any other sound or action. This corrective technique is one that teaches rather than terrorizes. It is designed to communicate to the dog that he is doing something wrong and the extra step of what he should be doing. The leash and collar are problematic. One must choose whether to let them remain on the animal most of the time so that he can be rushed outside without delay or to have them standing by in a convenient place. Taking a dog outside in the middle of his digestive release requires that you have speed and agility.

2. Feeding and Walking Schedule. The following schedule must be strictly adhered to for the entire housebreaking period. The training period should last only between two and four weeks, the feeding and walking schedules should then be adjusted according to the needs of the dog and the convenience of the owner. As the dog gets older, change his schedule to the one that applies to his age range. You will find that in most cases the number of feeding times recommended per day is consistent with those suggested by professional dog people. Seek the advice of a veterinarian for the specific needs and requirements of your dog.

The following schedule will work if the dog owner does not allow the dog the freedom of the house unless he or she is there to watch for the signs of the need to eliminate. When the dog is not supervised he must be confined to one enclosed area. (See Confinement to One Area, page 153.)

FEED-WATER-WALK SCHEDULES

Puppies Seven Weeks to Six Months Old

7:00 A.M.	Walk the dog.
7:30 A.M.	Feed, water, and walk.

11:30 A.M.	Feed, water, and walk.
4:30 P.M.	Feed, water, and walk.
8:30 P.M.	Water and walk (no more water after this time).
11:00 P.M.	Walk only.

Puppies Six to Twelve Months Old

7:00 A.M.	Walk the dog.
7:30 A.M.	Feed, water, and walk.
12:30 P.M.	Water and walk.
4:30 P.M.	Feed, water, and walk.
7:30 P.M.	Water and walk (no more water after this time).
11:00 P.M.	Walk the dog.

Dogs Twelve Months and Older

7:00 A.M.	Walk the dog.
7:30 A.M.	Feed, water, and walk.
4:30 P.M.	Water and walk.
7:30 P.M.	Water and walk (no more water after this time).
11:00 P.M.	Walk the dog.

The success of these schedules depends on absolute consistency. Feed, water, and walk your dog according to the schedule that applies to your dog. Provide your dog with all the water he wants before his walk. Do not feed him other than what he gets at the scheduled times. By scheduling your dog's intake of food and water you succeed in regulating his digestive process. It is important that you not allow the dog to remain outdoors for exercise when he is being walked for housebreaking purposes. If you walk the dog for a long period of time either before or after he eliminates he will never fully understand the point of the walk. Walking for exercise should be eliminated during the housebreaking training. Give the animal a long, supervised play period indoors instead.

Obviously, no young dog or puppy will be able to hold in his need to empty when first beginning this schedule. The solution is to confine the animal to an area, while you are at work, where he can urinate or defecate without causing damage to the house. Place newspapers over that entire area and never correct the dog for messing there. Take up the papers the minute you arrive home and allow the dog to run around the house providing you watch him for mistakes.

3. Proper Diet. Many of the most scientific studies of small-animal nutrition have been made by the commercial dog-food manufacturers. The result has been the marketing of superior commercial dog food. The proper balance of vitamins, minerals, proteins, carbohydrates, and fats is essential to the well-being of your dog. These essentials can be obtained from a combination of meat (fresh or canned) and commercial cereal-type dog foods. It is best to feed your dog high quality, premium dog food, especially during the house training. Under no circumstances should leftovers from your dinner table constitute the dog's diet. For one thing, it encourages the dog to beg for food while you are eating. And, most important of all, there is no way to know for sure that the animal is getting all the nutrients he requires.

Once you have settled on the proper diet for your dog do not vary from it. It will have a direct bearing on the success of the housebreaking. No food or doggie treats should be given to the dog between his feeding times. Avoid the temptation if you want this training to work. And, finally, allow the young puppy an extra walk if he consumes a large amount of water after a playful run around the house.

4. Getting Rid of the Odor. Most dogs return to the same area (sometimes the same spot) to urinate or defecate. They are attracted to the smell that still lingers, even if humans can't detect it. When the puppy or mature dog has an accident in any area of the house—even his own—the spot must be deodorized thoroughly so that he is not drawn back to his own scent. It is important not to allow scent posts to be established anywhere indoors. It is important in housebreaking that the dog's odors be obliterated from the floor. This can only be accomplished with the use of an odor neutralizer. There are many such products available in pet supply outlets and catalogs. One of the most efficient is called Nilodor. This is a highly concentrated odor neutralizer. Only a few drops placed directly over the soiled area, a fast mopping, and the scent is eradicated. The dog's smelling mechanism is much more efficient than we realize; he can smell odors that humans can't. For that reason do not rely on plain soap and water, ammonia (which smells like urine), bleach, or detergents to rid the floor of the dog's urine scent. You must use an odor neutralizer. The dog will begin to mess indoors less frequently once his odors cease to exist in the house. This must be accomplished each and every time the dog has an accident.

5. Confinement to One Area. The only answer to avoiding a ruined home is to confine the dog in an area that is least offensive to you when he has accidents. With the exception of very young puppies, most dogs will try to avoid messing in an area that is close to where they have to eat and sleep. Puppies have almost no control and will not be able to help themselves. The area of confinement should be where the dog eats and sleeps. The kitchen is probably the most suited for this purpose for several reasons. The kitchen floor is usually non-porous which has the benefit of not being ruined by urine. By applying a see-through gate in the kitchen doorway the dog is out of the way and yet is able to still feel that he has not been locked away from everything and everyone. The area should be provided with an accordion or pressure gate rather than a closed door so the dog does not feel that he has been punished or banished from his home.

The area of confinement can also be a dog crate which is a wire rectangle with a metal or wood floor and can be purchased in a size suitable for each dog. If used properly it ties in directly with your dog's instincts to have a den as the core area of his territory. A puppy or adult dog that is being house-trained should remain in the crate whenever he cannot be supervised. However, a dog should not remain in a crate for more than two or three hours at a time. The exception to this rule is at night. A dog or puppy can be crated for the entire night without being considered inhumane.

When you come home release the dog from his confinement and do not punish him if he has messed on the floor. Remember, you can correct the dog only if you catch him doing it. Once you are home, allow the dog to run loose but keep a close watch over him. If he gets out of your sight and messes on the floor there is nothing you can do and you will have wasted one entire day of housebreaking training. Be in a position to correct the dog and run him outside the minute he starts to relieve himself.

Paper-Training

*Paper-training is a technique for conditioning a dog to relieve himself **indoors**, on the floor, in a specific location that is covered with newspapers, and nowhere else.*

It is important to decide as early as possible whether to housebreak or paper-train your dog. With a few exceptions, you are certain to confuse your dog if you attempt to housebreak him (relieve himself outdoors) and paper train him (relieve himself indoors) at the same time. This is often the case with new puppy owners.

In some situations, the veterinarian advises new puppy owners to confine their young dogs indoors until all of their shots are completed. This could last for six months. After that, housebreaking can commence, but not without making the training more difficult. Although beginning housebreaking after paper-training is not impossible, it will take longer with more mistakes made by the dog.

Paper-training your dog is not very difficult. Everything written about housebreaking applies to paper-training, with the exception of a few important differences pertaining to the papers on the floor. If possible, do not attempt to housebreak and paper-train your dog at the same time.

Ten Easy Steps to Paper-Training Your Dog

1) Select a place *indoors* that is a suitable location for your dog to relieve himself. The kitchen floor is the most typical place because of its convenience and because of the nonporous floor covering that is usually there. Once you decide on a location, you must consistently use that one and no other.

2) Cover the floor of the entire toileting area with newspapers so that the dog cannot possibly make a mistake when he is taken there to relieve himself.

During the training period, spread out less paper each day so that the dog is only utilizing one portion of the floor by the end of the week. This not only saves paper, it narrows down the toileting area to manageable proportions. As in housebreaking, the dog is guided to his papered area in a direct route and should be allowed access according to the papering schedule provided in this section of the chapter. If convenient, it is best to have papers on the floor, ready at all times *during the training period only*.

If the dog has difficulty in the beginning of training and does not understand why you have placed him on the papers, save one soiled sheet of paper each time he relieves himself. Place it on top of the fresh paper when you are ready to have the dog use the papers again. His own scent will attract him and stimulate his need to relieve himself.

3) Until the dog is paper-trained, confine his movements in the house to one room when no one is there. Remember, when you paper-train a dog you are teaching him to relieve himself on the floor of your home. If you do not confine his activity to one place, he will use the floor no matter where he is in your home, whether there is paper or not. You may confine the dog in the same room that you paper him in, such as the kitchen, providing that you do not have papers on the floor except at the time provided by the papering schedule. The floor must always be clean.

If the dog is allowed out of the restricted area, watch him closely for signs that he must "go." The best place to confine your dog is a room where he can see what's going on, such as your kitchen. Other areas of confinement are the bathroom (with the door open), the garage, the basement, or in a closed-off hallway. The floor of the confinement area should be covered with linoleum or some other nonporous material in case the dog has "accidents." Always allow the dog to see what is going on by confining him with a see-through puppy gate. Otherwise, confining him is going to seem like punishment, which is the wrong effect.

4) Take the dog to his newspapers first thing in the morning and last thing in the evening, after each meal, and

after drinking water. (See the papering schedule following this schedule.)

5) Praise is an extremely useful teaching tool in paper-training. Lavishly praise your dog immediately after he relieves himself on the papers at his toileting area *when he performs on schedule*. Let him know that his using that one, consistent location really pleases you. The idea is to motivate the dog to do the right thing. Almost all dogs will work hard for your approval.

6) During the period that you are paper-training your dog, take him off his newspapers immediately after he has used them for their intended purpose. Do not allow him to misinterpret why he is there. It is not for play or recreation, otherwise he will give you false signals just to get you to take him there. During the training period the paper area must be used strictly for business.

7) When the dog is allowed to be out of his confined area in the house, you must watch for the signs that he has to relieve himself. This is especially important if your dog is a puppy. The signals for relieving himself are when he sniffs around the ground in an intense manner. When he starts to turn around in circles you have only seconds to stop him and carry him to the papering area. Adolescent and fully grown dogs may actually come and get you and stare hard in your eyes or go to the paper area and look at you. When that happens you have a near-paper-trained dog that is worth his weight in gold, and you must always respond to that signal.

8) Feed your dog on a consistent schedule so that his need to eliminate will also be on a consistent schedule. If you plan to put him on a self-feeding program, do not start it until he is completely paper-trained. (See the papering schedule following this section.)

9) Do not punish your dog if he has an accident. If you catch him in the act, say "NO" in a firm tone of voice and rush him to his papering area. You can also use a soda can with some pennies inside and use that as a noise correction device. Shake the can loudly and say "NO" if the dog is making a mistake. Do not do this once the dog has already made the mistake. Under no circumstances should you hit your dog or rub his nose in his own mess. You may feel better, but it only teaches your dog to fear you and has nothing to do with paper-training. As in obedience training, mistakes are to be "corrected" with a positive teaching method rather than a punishing, negative aspect.

10) When you come home to find that your dog has had an "accident," it is best to obliterate the odor to prevent him from returning to it and repeating his transgression. Once a dog urinates or defecates on a specific place, he can smell it later and feels compelled to "mark" it again and again. By eliminating that odor, which will be imperceptible to humans, you will prevent him from repeating his mistake. The only way you can completely eliminate such an odor from your dog's highly developed smelling capability is by using a concentrated odor neutralizer. There are several adequate products available at pet supply dealers.

Using a Dog Crate for Paper-Training

A dog crate is a metal enclosure made of thick wire with a metal or wood floor and can be purchased in a size suitable for any dog. It is only a cage with a door if that is how you choose to consider it. But to your dog it represents a den or core area within his territory. To a dog, a crate is a sanctuary. *From the dog's view it is not so much that he cannot get out but rather that you cannot get in.* However, the crate is much more than a sanctuary. It is an extremely useful tool when paper-training your dog—whether he is a puppy, adolescent, or adult animal.

Paper-training a puppy begins the day he comes into your home. It can take as little as three days and as long as three weeks. During the period of paper-training the pup should not have the run of the house without being carefully watched. Crate the dog at all times when no one is home to watch him and keep him out of trouble. His inclination not to soil his den will work for you if you place the little dog on a schedule that takes into account his tiny bladder and poor control over his eliminating needs.

Place the puppy on a strict FEED-WATER-PAPER-CON-FINEMENT schedule. Adhere to the established schedule consistently so as to regulate the dog's digestive system.

FEED-WATER-PAPER-CONFINEMENT SCHEDULE for Puppies*

Early morning	Paper the dog and return to confinement area.
Immediately afterwards	Feed, water, paper, and return to confinement area.
Mid-morning	Water, paper, and return to confinement area.
Past noon	Feed, water, paper, and return to confinement area.
Mid-afternoon	Water, paper, and return to confinement area.
Late afternoon	Water, paper, and return to confinement area.

Early Evening	Feed, water, paper, and return to confinement area.
Before Bed	Paper the dog and return to confinement area for the night. No water.

All dogs need to be walked for exercise and socializing. Walk young puppy or adult dog any time he has used his papers.

* When paper-training an adult dog, eliminate any inappropriate feeding from the schedule.

7

MISBEHAVIOR

Sometimes a dog misbehaves and upsets his family with actions and responses that are inappropriate for the human environment. Misbehavior often confuses pet owners as they try to cope with their dog's misdeeds. When a dog doesn't behave, many believe it is a dog problem. This reference is sometimes misleading and not very helpful.

Dogs can be defined by a very specific set of behavioral characteristics which have evolved over tens of thousands of years into a set of inherited actions and responses. Normal dog behavior is, to a large extent, predictable. What is not predictable is the impact on the behavior of dogs from their environmental influences. Once a dog has been exposed to human contact during the earliest phase of puppyhood, his desire to become part of the human family is great. Living the life of a family dog makes him happy and responsive to the people with whom he comes in contact. It is, to a large degree, why he behaves. Such a dog can be a true companion and friend and makes good company for everyone.

A dog that defends its home aggressively will not attack a stranger when introduced properly by the owner. This is *predictable* dog behavior. But if that same animal were abused in any serious manner or traumatized by an event, in addition to not being obedience trained, its behavior with a stranger would be *unpredictable* no matter what the owner might say or do. The dog's behavior would then be attributable to a *human* problem and could not logically be called a *dog* problem.

Can a dog remain true to his sweet and magical self when conditions are imposed on him that go against his nature? Dogs are almost always expected to deny their own natural responses in the human world and readjust their behavior to suit human demands made upon them. Such circumstances can create depressed dogs, aggressive dogs, destructive dogs, phobic dogs—and that's only the tip of the iceberg that can pervade an otherwise happy household. When dogs become destructive or refuse to be housebroken, the family must confront the issues and figure out what to do.

When your dog misbehaves, the solutions to his problems are as different and unique as one dog is from another. There are no set answers to any behavioral difficulties in dogs. What works for one will not necessarily work for another. The family should reject preconceived ideas, old wives tales, and free advice offered over the back fence unless it comes from experienced dog owners or working professionals.

Assuming the relationship with your dog is important, the solutions for behavioral problems require effort, patience, and understanding. You must be able to evaluate a dog's misbehavior as normal or abnormal . . . for a dog. All too often a dog will seem to be behaving strangely. However, its behavior, which has been formed over the ages by nature, may be absolutely correct for its species, despite the fact that it conflicts with human values. What is required of the dog owner is a working knowledge of dog behavior so that elements in the environment which stimulate unpleasant behavior can be eliminated, changed, or at the very least, understood. Of course, some dog behavior can be modified by using various behavior-changing techniques directly on the dog. If an animal's behavior is evaluated as abnormal when compared to its true nature, there is little the average person can do, outside of getting professional help. Extreme aggressiveness, shyness, and various phobias are among the abnormal behaviors requiring outside help. Some problems can be solved by professional dog trainers; others require the services of specialists working with behavior modification. Fortunately, most canine misbehavior can be dealt with by learning what is normal for a dog and why. With that information, you can either alter the dog's living conditions or modify the dog's behavior using direct techniques. (If you have not yet done so, please read Chapter Two, "The Canine Response," to better understand the material in this chapter.)

Puppies

The pleasures derived from puppies more than compensate for their constant piddling on the carpet and the sting of their sharp, needle-like teeth. If you want to understand your puppy you must understand the dog that he will grow into. Understanding your little dog helps avoid destructive anger as you attempt to find solutions and answers to the tail-wagging baby's misbehavior.

As in human infancy, the early phase of a dog's life involves physical growth and mental development. Human childhood is a long phase of development, perhaps the longest in nature, and under the best circumstances involves two adult parents protecting, providing for, and instructing the child. It goes on for at least eighteen years (and longer).

For dogs, infancy to adulthood is compacted into one year.

In the first three weeks of puppyhood, the young dog develops all of his sensory abilities plus many of his motor capacities. From the beginning of the fourth week until the end of the seventh week, the puppy enters a period of socialization the consequences of which affect his behavior for the rest of his life. During this critical period of socialization, the dog's environment plays a major role in how the animal will be able to adapt to human beings (and the demands they make) and the presence of other dogs. During this four-week period, the brain and the central nervous system are developing into full maturity. Interaction with litter mates and the mother teach the puppy indelible lessons about "pack existence." This canine socialization helps them create attachments to other puppies and produces an animal that will adjust easily to other dogs as an adult. If, in addition, the puppy is handled by a human being at least once a day between four and seven weeks of age, the dog will also adapt readily to humans with ease and comfort. Thus, by the end of the seventh week, the animal will become adaptive to dogs and humans and will get along well with both, as well as accept future dog training successfully. It is then time to remove the puppy from the litter before the question of dominance and subordination is settled within the litter.

Beginning in the eighth week, some pups start to bully others, while some become timid, shy, and even terror-ridden. The issue of who is dominant and who is subordinate is settled by puppy fights, the competition for food, and best placement for the mother's body warmth. The largest male often becomes the dominant animal at the expense of the other dogs who in turn work out their dominant or subordinate relationships with each other. These placements in the pack structure become permanent in the minds of the dogs. If the litter remains together for up to sixteen weeks, the order of dominance and subordination becomes set. Often a dominant dog will become an overly aggressive animal, untrainable or unsuitable for a pet/human relationship. An undersized puppy may be last in the pack structure and develop into an extremely timid or shy animal which has negative consequences when he becomes an adult dog living as a pet.

Between eight and sixteen weeks, personality based on dominance and subordination takes shape. In a pack environment, the young dog takes his place in the social structure until circumstances dictate the necessity for change. Anytime after six months, a dog is physically capable of mating and renewing the cycle. When a human family takes a puppy into their home, this cycle is still ongoing, with the human environment substituting for the canine factors. Ideally, a pet dog should take a subordinate position in relation to his family (or pack). This can come about only if the dog is adaptive to humans and if the humans in the family take the leadership position (without becoming overbearing). When the pet owner understands this, he or she is prepared for what comes naturally. In the beginning, all puppy behavior is based on instinct and the predilection toward pack structure. With this knowledge in mind you are better prepared to cope with your dog's misbehavior.

Puppy Problems

Crying All Night. Puppies do not cry through the first nights in a new home simply because they are willful or self-centered. A domestic dog's instincts are similar to those of his wild cousin, the wolf. If any wild *canid* should accidentally be separated from the litter or pack as a young pup, its life would be in grave jeopardy. The pup would be vulnerable to natural enemies. It would probably die of hunger since it is too young to hunt for food. From the dog's perspective, the first nights in a human situation are fraught with terror. He doesn't know where he is or what is going to happen. Everything familiar is gone. He has been taken away from his litter mates, his mother, his kennel, or the short-lived familiarity of a pet shop environment.

In the few hours spent with his new family, the dog has learned that he is safe in the human presence. When they leave him for the night, his fear of the unknown and his need for mother's warmth take over and cause him to howl. This is precisely why the puppy yells until he gains human attention. Unfortunately, that attention is often as unpleasant for the little dog as it is for the human. Too much howling usually earns him an unpleasant reaction from his new family. Unfortunately, he is often hollered at or hit.

Removed from his familiar territory, his litter mates, his mother and even his new pack the puppy feels lost and abandoned in his new home. Although it is not necessary to allow the puppy to sleep in the same bed, it is humane to soothe the dog and try to alleviate his fears. There are several ways to do this. The best method is to use a large cardboard box or wire dog crate as a means of bedding the dog in a confined area. Use a high-sided carton so that he cannot crawl out. Place the box with the dog in it in your bedroom each night so that the puppy is constantly aware of your presence.

This method is effective for two reasons. First, in the first three or four weeks of the puppy's life, he has no physical ability to eliminate his body wastes. Elimination is accomplished through stimulation by the mother's tongue as she licks her puppies' stomachs. In those early weeks the puppies learn that no body wastes are allowed to fall into their nest. The mother ingests them, thus maintaining a state of hygiene. By the fourth week, all the puppies leave the nest to eliminate independently. They never relieve themselves inside the nest (if they can help it). This imprinted behavior will be carried over into the puppy's new environment. While in the nest he is more likely to control his body functions, at least to the extent that he is physically able. (Please refer to Chapter Six, "House-Training Your Dog.")

Second, within a very short period of time (sometimes within hours), your new puppy bonds with you and your family as his new litter (or pack). Therefore, sleeping in the same room is very natural to him.

Another reason for confining the puppy in a small box is so that he cannot circle around with ease as he does before he defecates. If you decide to allow the puppy's nest to be placed in your bedroom, it is a good idea to close the door just in case he manages to climb out of the carton. A free-roaming puppy will use the entire house for his toilet and may get himself into serious trouble. Because a puppy's stomach and bladder are small, he may have one or two accidents throughout the night, but at least the mess will be confined to the box, providing he cannot crawl out of it. It may be a good idea to spread newspapers around the bedroom just in case the puppy does get out and relieves himself. This will not conflict with housebreaking (which does not involve newspapers).

Another way of comforting a puppy so that he will not be too distressed during those awful first nights is to place a ticking alarm clock in the box with him. This simulates his mother's heartbeat and has some good effect. A half-filled hot water bottle wrapped in a towel may feel like one of his litter mates is with him and offer a soothing effect. A dog's sense of smell is his keenest sense. Therefore, a towel or blanket that has the odor of his last home will be of enormous help in this distressing situation. Dogs remember many things by cataloging odors in their memories. The smell of their last home may be of great comfort. If the puppy is going to be confined in another room, play a radio on low volume or a one-hour recording of your voice on a tape cassette. This, too, may calm the little animal so that all may get a night's sleep.

Chewing. Chewing problems can be the result of boredom, anxiety or loneliness. Most often, however, it is the puppy's response to pain caused by teething. As the young dog loses its twenty-eight "milk teeth," forty-two permanent teeth erupt through the gums around the fifth month of life and give the young dog some trouble. Chewing hard objects seems to offer some form of relief from the pain and itching. Unfortunately, the chewing is usually destructive to human property and can result in a chewing habit that continues throughout the dog's life unless it is corrected. The best approach is to ease the young dog's discomfort by providing suitable chew toys made of digestible materials. A good approach is to give the dog a small dish with a few ice cubes in it. The cold temperature numbs the gums a bit and soothes them. Along the same lines, moisten a couple of clean washcloths, squeeze the water out of them, twist them into a rope-like shape and put them in the freezer of your refrigerator. Offer them to the dog as a soothing chew toy once they are frozen. Never give a puppy a chew toy that resembles a real object that you would not want him to chew. Old shoes and socks have the same bad effect. They teach the puppy to chew those items later, as a grown dog.

Nipping and Biting. Make no mistake about it, this is not cute or endearing misbehavior. It foreshadows very serious problem behavior if not dealt with early on. Nipping and biting problems are intolerable and must be discouraged the moment they begin. The nip of a puppy may tickle, but when that youngster grows into a dog it can tear a muscle or even break a human bone with its teeth and powerful jaws. Nipping often begins with teething or it may be related to the inherited temperament of the dog. More than likely it is behavior that was encouraged and possibly taught by humans during puppyhood. Keep your fingers out of the puppy's mouth. It is not a proper way to play with a puppy. A finger in her mouth teaches her to bite. It can become a horror later on. Each and every time a puppy nips or bites you (or anyone else) correct her. Say, "NO" in a firm tone of voice. The instant the pup stops her negative action, praise her. Say, "GOOD DOG" in a congratulating way and pet her. (See "Praise and Correction" in Chapter Five, "Getting Your Dog Under Control.")

Barking. Barking is another serious problem that must be stopped as it begins in puppyhood. The small yipping of a sweet baby dog soon becomes full-throated barking and howling, and can get your neighbors quite angry. There are hundreds of precedents set by judges ordering tenants to get rid of their dogs or vacate their premises. Excessive barking is no joke. Sometimes dogs are encouraged to bark by receiving a favorable response to this behavior. It is bad enough if you have a breed with a predisposition toward barking, such as those of the terrier group. But to laugh when a puppy barks in response to your command is asking for future trouble. You are then teaching a dog to bark, actually rewarding him for it, and also encouraging him to "talk back" when given a command. It is a violation of the dominant role you are supposed to assume. Avoid this at all costs. It is much easier to teach a dog not to bark as a puppy than to try to solve the problem later on. Vigorous daily exercise often stops a chronic barker from disturbing the neighbors when you are gone.

When your puppy barks say, "NO" in a firm tone of voice. When he stops, say, "GOOD DOG" in a congratulatory tone of voice. Then pet him. (See "Praise and Correction" and "How To Administer a Leash Correction" in Chapter Five, "Getting Your Dog Under Control.")

Out of Control. A puppy out of control does as he pleases, while ignoring you and everyone else in the family. This behavior leads to all sorts of mischief and misbehavior including piddling everywhere, chewing everything and everyone, barking, and indulging in all sorts of destructive activities.

If it is clearly established from the beginning that your puppy is a subordinate member of the family and that you are the dominant figure, your training problems will be reduced, as will many negative behavior situations. This means that every human in your household must also be in a dominant position in relation to the little dog. Wolves and dogs are insecure without a leader and will fill that role if necessary. A dominant dog might chew up the house, bite a visitor, deliberately vomit, or otherwise soil the house in an escalating attempt to gain something it neither understands nor can achieve, which is control of the situation.

Do not confuse being dominant with your puppy with being violent or abusive in any way. Hitting a dog or even hollering at him never achieves the positive results you want. It can make your puppy aggressive, fear-aggressive, or alienate him from you. Abusive behavior with your dog does not teach him anything except to fear you. Never hit your dog.

The way to gain the dominant position with him is easy. Teach the dog that your commands are consistent and that you mean what you say. If you say to the puppy, "NO" when he heads for the garbage can, follow it through and carry him or shoo him away. Do not say "NO" and then let him do what he wants anyway. In this situation call the puppy to you in a playful manner. As he runs to you, turn around and walk in the opposite direction. Make the puppy follow you. When he catches up, bend down and pet him and tell him what a good dog he is. Repeat this many times during the day until the dog comes to you every time you call him. What you are teaching him is to come when called. (See "Teaching the Recall" in Chapter Five, "Getting Your Dog Under Control.") This is the manner in which you must teach this command while your dog is still a puppy. It works beautifully. However, it is essential that you never call your puppy to you in order to holler at him or hit him, or even correct. If you do that he will stop coming to you when you call him. Anyone would.

The tone of your voice is another way of taking the dominant role and gaining control over your puppy. A firm, no-nonsense tone tells the puppy and adult dog that you must be obeyed. Do not confuse a firm tone of voice with shrieking hysteria. It is not recommended that you holler at your dog. It will terrorize him and do irreparable damage to your relationship with him. Giving the young puppy a call name as soon as possible allows you to gain the dominant position quickly and apply these techniques. The guideline to successful dog training is gaining the dog's confidence and trust, while behaving in a leader-like manner.

An interesting technique for gaining dominance over a puppy or young dog is to place a leash and collar on the animal. Then, tie the end of the leash onto your belt loop or pin it to your waist in some fashion. For the next thirty minutes or so simply have the dog follow you around the house as you do your chores or move about. This achieves interesting results, providing you are assertive (not overpowering), friendly (not gushing), and decisive (not dictatorial). When you move, bear in mind that the young dog cannot move as fast as you and will be a bit bewildered in the beginning. Talk to him as you go about your home from place to place. Entice him to follow you, for that is the point to the exercise: People lead, dogs follow! Use common sense and good judgment about how long to do this and how often.

Adult Dog Problems

At the end of the first year most breeds are approaching their full height and weight and are what they will be for the rest of their lives, both mentally and physically. Your dog's curiosity and audacity will be at full peak and (if you have behaved properly) he will be fully confident of his place in the family structure. It is hoped that his subordinate position has been well established, and that he is a happy dog with that arrangement.

By the twelfth month, a dog is definitely an adult by any standard (with the exception of the giant breeds). Of course, he still has many adolescent traits that will fade away like a child's old toys, providing you do the right thing. At this age the dog is still capable of creating mischief and must be firmly dealt with if and when he tries to take the dominant position in the household. Although your dog is now a fully accepted member of the family and sometimes behaves like a human being, he must not be treated like a human being. Treating your dog like the wonderful dog that he is will do just fine.

The Dog Crate

Despite popular wisdom, a dog crate is not a jail. This is a common misconception that some dog owners have about the wire dog crate. A dog crate is not a cage to prevent him from getting out but, from the dog's point of view, it is to keep you from getting in.

A dog crate is usually a wire rectangle with a Masonite floor, although it can be made of an assortment of materials. Crates are available in many different sizes, tailored for various dog breeds. It only *looks* like a cage with a door. If used properly, it ties in directly with your dog's instincts to have a den as the core area of his territory. A dog crate is a sanctuary for your pet, a home within his home.

The crate is the ideal haven for any dog or puppy when your home looks and sounds like a carnival. During times of stress, a dog crate is a soothing place to relax and calm down. But the crate is actually much more than a sanctuary. It is a very useful *indoor* tool when housebreaking or paper-training your dog, because his instinct is to keep his den clean. Place the crate in a small, closed-off area, such as the kitchen with the door left open and newspapers placed nearby. Your puppy will sleep in the crate as a den, especially if you provide a blanket. Once he adjusts to this arrangement, he will show better bowel control by eliminating only once or twice, when taken outdoors. Allow for "accidents." After this period of adjustment, your puppy can be crated all night in his regular daytime place. He will avoid making mistakes all over your floors if the crate door is closed until morning.

Another time that the crate is useful is during your new dog's chewing period. All puppies and young dogs chew whatever they can get into their mouths because of teething pain, lack of attention, anxiety, boredom, fear, or insufficient opportunity to use up excess energy. Crating your puppy can prevent household damage from destructive behavior. But the crate must be used in connection with a sensible solution to the primary cause of the problem, such as lack of exercise, the need for medical treatment, more loving attention, etc.

A dog crate can be part of a general obedience training program or a way of confining your puppy when his behavior is annoying. Crating can help keep him out of mischief whether someone is home or not. However, the dog must form a positive association with the crate and never a frightening one. It must never be used for punishing your dog.

Make the crate cozy so that it is your dog's *indoor* doghouse. Place a few harmless chew toys inside for distraction, or a towel or familiar blanket. Set the crate up near an area of family activity—the kitchen or a main hallway. Drape a cloth over the top and sides to create a doghouse atmosphere. Some trainers place a small food reward at the back of the crate before confining the puppy inside. This helps create a pleasant feeling upon entering. Except at night, your puppy should never be crated for more than a few hours at a time. A crate should never be used all day as a convenience for a regularly absent pet owner. That would be inhumane and damaging to the dog's personality.

Another way to get a puppy to accept a crate is to establish a "crating routine." Place the puppy in the crate at regular one- to two-hour intervals during the day. Let your puppy's nap times guide you. The puppy can be crated for up to three or four hours if you are leaving the house. Give her a safe chew toy for distraction and remove her collar and tags, which could get caught in an opening.

The crating routine can be used during car travel with your dog or puppy. Depending on its size, the crate can fit into the back seat of the average car. Confined in the crate, your puppy cannot stick her head out the window or distract the driver. Most puppies accept the crate if they are exposed to it early and are not placed there in anger. However, some puppies never accept the idea. In that case, it is kinder and wiser to give up crating. If it works, crating is a useful technique and well worth trying because of the benefits to your dog and your family.

Barking. Nothing makes dog owners more ambivalent than the subject of barking. On the one hand, barking makes them happy because of the protection it offers as a deterrent to criminal trespassing. On the other hand, it is annoying and irritating to everyone, including unsympathetic neighbors who hate dogs and have a burglar alarm instead. So, the horn of the dilemma is that they want dogs to bark when it makes sense and to be silent when it does not. That is a tall order, which can only be achieved by a professional dog trainer who specializes in training dogs for guard work. And then there are dog owners who never want their dogs to bark under any circumstances, which is somewhat more realistic. All dogs bark at some point and it can never be eliminated altogether. However, this undesirable behavior can be reduced dramatically and gotten under control.

Barking is a natural part of dog behavior, although some breeds bark more than others. Barking is usually the result of a stimulus such as a stranger entering your property or the sound of a motorcycle zooming past the dog. It is, in essence, a form of canine communication triggered by agitation of some sort which can become generalized or habitual behavior. In other words, sometimes barking has a point to it and often it does not.

If your dog barks excessively, it may be because he is extremely aggressive, angry, lonely, playful, bored, stressed, protective, or frightened. A dog may bark because he is improperly confined (crated too long), isolated (dogs are social creatures, remember), chained to one place, stimulated by noise, hungry, cold, hot, taunted by children, or simply untrained and undisciplined. You may be able to reduce your dog's barking problem by changing the environmental cause. If not, you must engage in a form of behavior modification and try to solve the problem by altering his behavioral responses.

Solutions to the Barking Problem

1) If you do not want your dog to bark under any circumstances, you must communicate to him that he must stop this behavior. This is accomplished with leash corrections and praise. Have your dog obedience-trained. This gets him under control. An obedience-trained dog will respond properly to your commands, especially when you catch him in the act of misbehaving. Obedience training establishes the proper relationship of human dominance and canine subordination. You will not have to shout hysterically or lose control of yourself in order to take charge of your dog's behavior. (Please refer to Chapter Five, "Getting Your Dog Under Control.")

2) Learn how to administer a leash correction when you catch your dog barking. (See "The Leash Correction" in Chapter Five, "Getting Your Dog Under Control.") The most basic problem-solving technique to stop barking is to set your dog up in a situation where you know he will bark, so that you can correct him for his misbehavior.

Place a leash and training collar on him and leave the room or the house if the dog barks indoors. If he barks outdoors, then leave his sight, even if you have to walk a block away.

Once the dog begins to bark, swiftly enter the room (or the backyard), take hold of his leash and say "NO" several times, in a loud, firm tone of voice. As you do this, employ a leash correction, a firm snap and release of the leash, which tightens the training collar around the dog's neck for an instant and is then released. This must be followed by praise for the dog. The praise both reassures him that he is still in your good graces and also rewards him for stopping his barking. It reinforces the correction and is an essential aspect of the technique. (Follow the *correction* instructions for this technique properly, as outlined in Chapter Five.)

3) If your dog barks because of "separation anxiety," you must deal with the problem differently. Separation anxiety (which also causes chewing problems and various forms of destructive and escape behaviors) is a serious problem. A nervous, insecure dog will feel frightened and sometimes frantic when left alone. This is usually the case in dogs that are never left alone at all, when the bond between human and dog is intense and one-on-one, or after a long separation (usually after a business trip or vacation).

Another cause of separation anxiety is paying too much attention to the dog just before leaving him alone. In this situation the dog is over stimulated with expressions of love and play, raising his emotional pitch. Such dog owners must learn from the experience of human parents. Parenthood involves preparing a child for independence by allowing the child to separate in gradual stages over a long period of time. Pet owners must not engage their dogs in guilt-inspired excessive behavior just before leaving the dog behind. Hugs, kisses, food treats, and expressions of affection only build the dog up to a high emotional pitch and let him topple all the way down once the door closes. The dog becomes depressed, frustrated, and then frightened. Out of this comes barking, chewing, and frantic digging at the walls, the doors, and even the windows (in extreme cases).

Handle the problem in gradual stages by getting him used to being alone without all the fuss associated with leaving. If the dog is obedience trained, run him through his commands before you leave. SIT-STAY is the best exercise for a dog that suffers with separation anxiety. Leave the dog alone for short periods of time and then return without much fanfare. Do this often, but extend the time it takes you to return in each instance. Remember, do not make a big deal out of leaving. Say, "STAY. GOOD DOG," and then leave. Also, do not make a big fuss on your return. Simply say, "GOOD DOG," and pet him. Fussing too much with your dog before leaving him alone either creates the problem or worsens it.

4) Other solutions to the barking problem are to exercise your dog before leaving him alone. Give him a safe chew toy to gnaw on when he gets bored. Arrange to have a neighbor come over when the dog barks and give

him a verbal correction ("NO! [pause] THAT'S A GOOD BOY.") Have your dog walked by a professional dog walker in the middle of the day or have a friend, neighbor, or relative do it. Solve your dog's other misbehaviors, such as housebreaking, chewing, digging, etc. As is often the case, one misbehavior creates another, such as barking.

Begging. A dog that begs at the dining table or the kitchen table is more than just annoying, he is out of control. It is an obnoxious habit that can cause a dinner guest never to return to your home. Begging dogs usually sit on the floor, looking up with a pathetic, whimpering look on their faces. They appeal to your humanity and make you feel guilty if you don't slip them something off your plate. Sometimes they stand on their hind legs and steal food from your plate. No matter how cute it may seem, begging for food is not to be tolerated. It indicates that your dog does not behave properly.

It is important to understand that eating between meals may upset the nutritional balance provided by your premium commercial dog food and could also cause obesity and other digestive disorders. Giving in to a begging dog's whimpers, stares, and pathetic expressions encourages him to become demanding which often leads to bullying and aggressiveness. It is a behavioral problem and should be stopped.

Hunger is not the only issue for a dog that begs. He will beg even if he has just finished eating. Giving him your food is a throwback to puppyhood when all dogs are cared for by their mothers. It represents a time of dependency and helplessness. It is immature behavior and a sign of underdevelopment. When a dog begs he not only wants your food, he wants your total involvement. It is a form of attention-getting that is not reasonable.

If you want your dog to behave like an adult, you must insist that he eats his own food from his own bowl and deny him the indulgence of begging. Even though a pet dog never has to fend for himself, he does need some forms of nurturing, just like the rest of us. However, he can continue to live the good pet-life without the unnecessary habit of begging. Emotional nurturing does not necessarily involve food.

Dogs beg because they are allowed to come to the table when the family is eating; they are fed table scraps; they are maintained on an inadequate diet; kept on an irregular feeding schedule; and given too little positive attention and affection.

Solutions to the Begging Problem

1) The first step you must take is deciding whether or not you want your dog to beg at your table. Decide now. Is it to be allowed or not? If you do not consider this a problem, skip the rest of this section. If you do not like this misbehavior then continue reading this section.

2) Feed your dog in a different part of the house than the dining room so that there can be no mistake about his territory. It should be in a place that is distinctly separate from yours. Never allow your dog to claim the dining area as his territory. If this has already happened, change these conditions.

3) If your dog has not yet been obedience-trained, it is time to do it. This gets him under control. An obedience trained dog will respond properly to your commands, especially when you catch him in the act of misbehaving. Obedience training establishes the proper relationship of

human dominance and canine subordination. You will not have to shout hysterically or lose control of yourself in order to take charge of your dog's behavior. (Please refer to Chapter Five, "Getting Your Dog Under Control.")

4) Correct your dog when he misbehaves. Whether you live with a little beggar or a big beggar, the solution is the same. Allow the dog to do his worst and, at the appropriate time, execute a leash correction. This must be done every time the dog begs for food, no matter where it happens.

In order to properly execute a leash correction, you must place a leash and metal training collar on the dog five or ten minutes before each meal. Then ignore him. Serve the meal as usual but be prepared to administer a correction. When the dog starts to beg, do nothing until it reaches its peak, which could involve sitting, starring at you, whimpering, or attempting to steal food.

At the right moment, grab the leash (gather up about three feet of it in your hand) and quickly snap it to the right side of the dog. When snapping the leash, be firm but gentle, so that the collar causes no pain as it tightens around the dog's neck for an instant. Release the tension on the leash *immediately* following the snap.

Do not snap the leash forward or in any direction other than to the right. The dog feels the correction when the slip collar tightens for an instant around his neck. It is not painful, but it is negative and gives the dog a sense of rejection for his infraction of your rules. The tug must always be accompanied with a firmly stated, "NO!" It is essential that you praise the dog immediately following each correction.

It may not be necessary to use the leash correction. You may find that clapping your hands loudly and then firmly saying, "NO!" is sufficient.

Be sure to say "NO" in a firm, harsh tone of voice as you execute any of the corrections, immediately followed by verbal praise for having obeyed you.

If your dog is obedience-trained, an interesting alternative is to use some of the training commands when he starts begging. A verbal correction ("NO") and "DOWN-STAY" or "GO TO YOUR PLACE" will do nicely.

5) Never feed your dog *anything* from the table. Insist that this rule be followed by all members of your family and dinner guests. Consistency on this point is vital.

Biting. There are more than a few good reasons why it is of vital importance for all dog owners to recognize signs of canine aggression and then to do what is necessary to prevent a dog from biting. Obviously, no one wants the family pet to harm anyone. And no one relishes lawsuits and medical expenses for which owners of dogs that bite are almost always held liable, or the possibility of having to surrender a loved dog to local authorities.

Some dogs who bite do so to defend their territory, possessions, or position of dominance. These are referred to as *dominant-aggressive* dogs. Some breeds (and some individual dogs) defend their homes with greater vigor than others and consider their human beings as much their personal property as their food bowls. But, as any mailman can attest, dogs cannot always understand the difference between intruders and innocent strangers. An innocent stranger can be a child chasing a ball, a delivery man, or a visiting relative.

A dog will bite either out of aggression or fear. Interestingly, most bites come from dogs referred to as *fear-aggressive* dogs. Fear or shy biters are most often females, although male dogs can also be nervous and fear-ridden. Aggressive dogs view their victims as enemies to be defeated. Fear biters do their damage as a way of defending themselves against an anticipated harm or, in some cases, as an uncontrollable response to something that terrifies them. Biters may also be dogs who have been abused by humans or other animals, abandoned, tormented, taught to be vicious, or suffering from a medical problem (pain can be one reason for a dog to begin biting). A dog who has once been beaten will have a great fear of the human hand—and to put out one's hand to pet such a dog could well invite a nip, or worse.

A dog who growls and snarls at you from deep within his throat; chases people, bicycles or cars; snaps, nips, and bullies is a potential biter. Many dogs snarl if *anyone* goes near their food or possessions, including their owners.

All dog owners should observe and try to understand their pets' idiosyncrasies and learn how to spot early symptoms of aggressive and fear behavior—and then act quickly, before the dog actually bites someone.

If your dog is under ten months of age and has begun to nip and bite, it is not too late to deal with the problem on your own. Dog obedience training is the most important cure there is for dog biting. You could castrate a male dog that bites and achieve a reduction in the dog's aggressive behavior. However, it would take at least six weeks for the male sex hormone, testosterone, to leave the dog's body, resulting in a change in his behavior. A professional trainer could have the dog obedient by then, giving the owner a great deal of control. Castrating an aggressive male dog would certainly help correct his biting problem, but the dog would still need obedience training. Some dogs require both measures. Obedience training is the answer for correcting biting problems in female dogs.

When your dog bites someone, you are already six weeks too late.

A dog who bites is not an asset and must be dealt with as soon as possible in tough, uncompromising terms. If your dog is ten months or older, you must get help from a professional dog trainer. Do not attempt to handle the problem yourself, as it is too dangerous.

Solutions to the Biting Problem

1) Prevention is the first therapy to employ. If you know you have an aggressive dog, you must not place him in a situation where he can bite someone. A fear-aggressive dog should not be approached by strangers. Never stare directly into the eye of a fear-aggressive (or dominant-aggressive) dog, as it represents a physical challenge and often results in an attack. Never allow anyone to extend their hands toward the dog or to pet the dog. Even offering a closed fist for the dog to sniff could invite a snap or bite. Do not holler at or hit an aggressive dog. Such dogs have been know to bite members of their own families if stimulated improperly.

2) Have your dog obedience-trained. This gets him under control. An obedience-trained dog will respond properly to your commands, especially when you catch him in the act of aggressive behavior. Obedience training establishes the proper relationship of human dominance and canine subordination. You will not have to shout hysterically or lose control of yourself in order to take charge of your dog's behavior.

3) Learn how to administer a leash correction when you catch your dog being aggressive. (See Chapter Five, "Getting Your Dog Under Control.") The most basic problem-solving technique to stop nipping and biting behavior (*in dogs ten months old and younger*) is to correct the dog for his misbehavior.

Place a leash and training collar on him and give him access to those to whom he displays his aggressive behavior. If he is never aggressive in front of you as a rule, leave the room. When he exhibits his aggressive behavior, swiftly enter the room, take hold of his leash and say, "NO" several times, in a loud, firm tone of voice. As you do this, employ a leash correction, a firm snap and release of the leash, which tightens the training collar around the dog's neck for an instant and is then released. This must be followed by praise for the dog. The praise both reassures him that he is still in your good graces and rewards him for stopping his aggressive behavior. It reinforces the correction and is an essential part of the technique. (Follow the *correction* instructions for this technique properly, as outlined in Chapter Five.)

A word of caution here. This technique may not be safe when used on some dogs. It all depends on the age, size, and ferocity of your dog. Use common sense and seek professional help when it seems logical to do so.

4) Some fear-aggressive dogs only exhibit their aggression toward specific types of persons or situations. For example, they may only be aggressive toward children or toward people of other races or with men who walk with a limp. This information can be valuable to a dog trainer or other professional whom you have engaged to help you with this problem. The solution is often to modify the dog's behavior toward such specific types by introducing them in small, drawn-out ways and developing pleasant associations with them. This process takes time and expertise but can be very effective.

Boredom. You may be boring your dog. It is quite possible that your dog does not answer to your call, does not run to you when you come home, does not jump up with pleasure, does not even pant when you come home. Other signs of boredom may be abnormal loss of appetite, abnormal gain of appetite, a string of minor illnesses, destructive chewing, barking, or nipping fingers. With no apologies for oversimplification, boredom is a common ailment of many house pets.

The quality of a pet is no more or less than the quality of his lifestyle. Because you are the wonderful, humane animal lover that you are, it is assumed that the family dog is properly fed, groomed, exercised, and cared for medically. However, your dog's needs do not end there. As in marriage, child-rearing, and the maintenance of friendships, much more is required than simple, day-to-day comforts.

In some households, the dog is walked twice a day, fed, and forgotten. Some of our best friends live with those who work and leave the poor animal to his own devices for the better part of ten hours a day. For one who does not read, watch daytime TV, or jog, this is boring.

The most common symptoms of boredom (destructive chewing, biting, listlessness) often cause a dog and a human to part company. No one wants their home or themselves abused. Bear in mind that a bored dog is a boring dog to be with. The animal shelters and city pounds have become the springboards to oblivion for millions of abandoned or rejected pets. It is an aspect of pet ownership that few humans anticipate.

The nature and lifestyle of the dog is almost identical to that of the wild *canids* (wolves, coyotes, etc.). They are social creatures, genetically organized to live in packs or pairs. The dog or wolf pack is essentially a family of related and/or non-related canines, all living together in a very specific social organization. The social order is based on dominance and subordination. The largest and most aggressive of the pack assumes the position of leadership and makes all decisions for the rest. They hunt, claim territory, mate, and raise cubs, with each member of the pack performing the various necessary tasks according to his rank in the established order.

Play is a very important element in the growth and progress of a dog, wolf, or coyote. Play is the activity by which *canids* learn about hunting, escaping from danger, fighting, and exercising their bodies. It is fascinating how they indulge in all degrees of play throughout their lives. However, play is seldom a solitary activity for dogs, as it is for cats. For these reasons it is clear that a dog who has become bored has been alone too long—untouched, unrelated to, and not played with. It is counter to the dog's nature. As fish need water, dogs need people or other living creatures with which to play and relate. They need hands-on treatment offering affection and stimulation.

One of the most effective means of keeping a dog alert and stimulated is to take him out for more than his usual housebreaking walks. Take him on your errands, such as trips to the dry cleaner, the mailbox, and social visits with friends and neighbors. Use the obedience training techniques in Chapter Five and train your dog. Obedience training is not hard on a dog and occupies his mind. It is one of the few activities that brings dog and human together in a concentrated form of relating. An obedience-trained dog will also be able to travel anywhere you wish to take him. Probably the greatest benefit of obedience training is communication on a meaningful level. There is nothing happier than a dog who knows exactly what is expected of him.

Grooming sessions can be fun and have the added benefit of keeping your dog looking and feeling good. Baths, brushing, ear cleaning, and nail clipping are all tasks that will prevent boredom.

Keeping your dog both physically fit and mentally alert is another important and easy method for canine stimulation. Apart from the usual forms of exercise, such as running and jumping, a good Frisbee throw will please any dog. Allow the dog to get his teeth into it to avoid frustration and poor self-image. You might also purchase a solid, hard-rubber ball and use it to good advantage.

Pure-bred dog owners can research the history of their breed and learn for what function it was developed. For example, retrievers would love to carry your newspaper or a small package in their mouths. They were bred to assist duck hunters by retrieving the quarry in their mouths. Some dogs need a good swim. Working breeds such as Alaskan malamutes or Siberian huskies enjoy pulling carts, wagons, or just about anything that will move. Herding dogs will assume responsibilities and make decisions. Give them something to guard or care for. Pet owners who are away all day at work should consider getting a pet for their dogs. It only sounds absurd. If your dog doesn't have a murderous attitude toward cats (most don't) get him a kitten. Of course, a second dog is ideal, providing the original pet agrees. If possible, taking your dog to work is a delightful option for both you and the dog.

By giving your dog a purpose, relating to him as a being who needs stimulation, and establishing communication, you will improve the quality of his life. Boredom is the enemy and leads to misbehavior.

Destructive Chewing. Destructive dogs are hard to cope
with because we come to love them before we understand
their terrible potential. Of course a continual assault on your
possessions will take some of the bloom off those tender
feelings and allow a thought or two about adoption agencies
and a new home on a farm. But before you send the dog to
the farm there are several methods available to solve the
problem and they are worth trying, if only to protect your
own feelings of guilt and to avoid the awful fate awaiting
a disinherited house dog.

Unless your dog is a pathological chewer (and few are),
he may simply be easing the pain in his gums caused by
teething. If that's the case, read "Chewing" in the Puppy
section of this chapter. In any event, stop worrying; the
problem will soon end. Try not to think of your dog as a
juvenile delinquent but, rather, as an uneducated youth with
all of the problems connected with canine adolescence.

Dogs do their worst damage if they are anxiety-ridden,
if they are bored, if they are lonely, if they are frustrated,
or if they are teething. These are all solvable problems
and, among the corrective techniques available, the most
effective place to begin is with obedience training. You
may hire a professional dog trainer to come to your home
or take the dog to a training class. Or, you may use the
training techniques offered in Chapter Five, "Getting Your
Dog Under Control."

Solutions to the Destructive Chewing Problem

1) Have your dog obedience trained. This gets him under
control. An obedience-trained dog will respond properly to
your commands, especially when you catch him in the act

of behaving destructively. Obedience training establishes the proper relationship of human dominance and canine subordination. You will not have to shout hysterically or lose control of yourself in order to take charge of your dog's behavior.

2) Get a dog crate. Next to obedience training, using a dog crate during this period of destructive behavior is the most important step you can take. That's because you must first confine your puppy or grown dog when you are not there in order to prevent him from indulging his need to chew on your possessions.

3) Learn how to administer a leash correction when you catch your dog in the act of chewing. (See Chapter Five, "Getting Your Dog Under Control.") The most basic problem-solving technique to stop chewing behavior is to set the stage for a chewing situation so that you can correct your dog for his misbehavior.

Allow him access to the thing he likes to chew the most. Place a leash and training collar on him and leave the room (leave the house if necessary). When he goes to his favorite object and begins to chew on it, swiftly enter the room, take hold of his leash and say "NO" several times, in a loud, firm tone of voice. As you do this, employ a leash correction, a firm snap and release of the leash, which tightens the training collar around the dog's neck for an instant and is then released. This must be followed by praise for the dog. The praise both reassures him that he is still in your good graces and rewards him for stopping his destructive behavior. It reinforces the correction and is an essential part of the technique. Follow the *correction* instructions for this technique properly, as outlined in Chapter Five.

4) Another method for stopping chewing behavior is to coat the objects the dog likes to chew with something

unpleasant tasting, such as Tabasco sauce or a paste made of water and alum. There are also commercial pet products formulated for this problem. One such product is Bitter Apple™. This is a self-correcting method and is often effective. Of course, there is no reason why you cannot employ more than one method at the same time to stop this upsetting behavior.

5) Change your behavior with the dog. This pertains to chewing (and other misbehaviors) caused by "separation anxiety." Many dogs misbehave because of the intense negative emotions they experience when they are left behind in a lonely house. They simply cannot bear to be left alone, which is a condition that can be changed when handled properly.

All dogs are social creatures but some become so attached to their families (or to one member of the family) that it is painful for them to be separated. It creates intense fear or anxiety which, in turn, sets the stage for much misbehavior, such as barking, chewing, urinating and defecating, and intense attempts to escape by digging at doors and windows.

(See solution number 3 in "Solutions to the Barking Problem" in this chapter for more information.)

Eating Problems. The three sins of feeding your dog are too little, too much, and poorly balanced food. For full growth and proper functioning of all systems of the body, a dog requires a balance of protein, carbohydrate, fat, water, vitamins, and minerals. In the wild, this balance is achieved by capturing and devouring another animal. The first part of the downed prey that is consumed is the contents of the stomach which provides grains and/or vegetation. The flesh, the layered fat, and even the bones all contribute to the proper balance of protein, carbohydrate, and all the rest.

The dog's close relative, the wolf, doesn't eat every day, especially during the long, hard winter months. Locating the prey and then downing it requires a great deal of energy and exercise. When you couple this with the demands made on the body by exposure to outdoor weather conditions, it is easy to calculate that the wolf or wild dog expends almost as much energy to work for his food as the energy equivalent consumed from the meal itself. One rarely comes across a fat wolf. Overfed or poorly fed domestic dogs lead shorter, unhealthy, and unhappy lives than those fed a well-balanced maintenance diet based on premium dog food.

There is a large difference between a dog off his feed and one that is considered finicky. A dog that insists on one type of food over another is usually involved in some psychological game created and encouraged by a human. When a very young dog enters a human situation, it takes on many of the behavioral aspects of the environment, and that includes behavioral game-playing. When the finicky dog is fed along the lines of taste preference (usually more to do with the human's preference), he learns to manipulate human behavior by eating or not eating. Some finicky dogs have been programmed to expect an elaborate set of food and feeding conditions, and if his owner forgets just one element of the pattern the dog refuses to eat.

This distorts the true nature of the dog. However, it is safe to say that domestication itself is a distortion of the original lifestyle of dogs. In the wild, like wolves, they are drawn into packs. They must forage for food or strenuously hunt for sick or young herding animals. This means they do not necessarily eat every day, nor does every member of the pack eat equally well. When a large game animal is brought down, the pack leader is the first to eat and takes the largest, choicest portions. But there is logic to this behavior. The lead male wolf or wild dog returns to the den and disgorges a large quantity of undigested food for the lactating female and/or weaning puppies. Harder work and greater responsibility require more food.

Domestically, however, dogs are not the leaders of their packs, nor should they be. A domestic dog is fed by his human caretaker who is, in effect, his pack leader. Domestic dogs that dictate the terms of their feeding habits are behaving in an unnatural manner, considering their position in the pack (human family).

From September to March, wild *canids* are nomadic and follow the grazing herds as a source of food. Between April and August, they remain within the boundaries of a fixed territory and eat squirrels, rabbits, small rodents, birds, fish, berries, and small fruits. Food is never more than a means of satisfying nutritional needs within the body. It has nothing to do with pleasure (in human terms), culinary art, aesthetics, or any of the social graces. Further, in the wild, food has no emotional or psychological meaning. It does not relate to love, acceptance, guilt, emotional stability, sexual adequacy, or dependencies brought about through bribery or blackmail. These are distorted values given to food by human beings. Unfortunately, some domestic dogs are taught to respond to them by their human families. This represents a clash between the animal's natural feeding instincts and conditions imposed on dogs by their human owners. This can only lead to bad behavior, such as growling and biting over food, finicky behavior, and withholding affection (blackmail).

Some pet owners feed their dogs as a way to get their love and attention. Food is not love. Nor is it the currency of love. Allowing a bit of philosophy, love is an emotion requiring no qualifications or payments. It is either present or not. Heaping a dog's bowl with leftover roast beef, mashed potatoes, carrots, gravy, and fat trimmings does not mean that your dog is going to love you any more than he already does. It merely makes the animal an unhealthy love object who eats too much of the wrong food. Dog owners must be able to separate their own relationship with food from that of their dog. Dogs eat to live and not the other way around.

Dogs that will not eat at all are usually suffering from a physical ailment. There are those dogs, however, that go off their feed because of an emotional problem. A dog that is upset will usually eat less or stop eating altogether. The most luxurious life in the world will not compensate for what is the true reality of a dog's life. Many animals, including humans, will die in the face of plenty if they lose their status or position in their respective pack, herd, or society. There is strong evidence that all animals are either given or develop a role for themselves in their social frameworks. When an animal is denied that role because of failing health, defeat, or incompetence, he becomes a self-sentenced "lone wolf." This isolated creature wanders off on a meaningless journey from which there is no return. Allowing a loved pet to eat like a dog rather than a human is probably more valuable to the animal's health than the composition of the food itself.

The other side of the same coin is when the dog begins to get fat. Warfare ensues in the kitchen. When a dog is loved to an extreme degree by his family, he is often attacked daily with a deadly barrage of food from the refrigerator. In such cases the kitchen is the battlefield and eventually becomes the killing ground because obesity in dogs and humans has the same lethal effect. It gradually destroys good health. Obesity shortens the life span of an animal and louses up the quality of life as well. Medically speaking, your pet does not have to resemble a blimp to be considered obese. If a dog is 15 to 20 percent overweight, he is obese.

It is quite true that some members of a breed are simply larger specimens than others. Therefore, one must learn how to determine when a dog is carrying too much weight. Obviously, an obese dog is easily identified, like white socks with a tuxedo. They tend to stand out from the crowd. Detecting the overweight dog, however, requires a few guidelines.

Merely weighing the dog is not much help unless a veterinarian has already determined your pet's ideal weight range. If that is the case, then you should weigh your fat dog once a week. This is not very difficult. With most breeds this can be done by subtracting your own weight from the combined weight of you and your dog when you're both on the scale.

Each canine is different physically and does have variables that must be taken into account. These variables have to do with breed of dog, bone structure, sex, working conditions, living conditions, weather conditions, and other environmental factors. These all help determine what the ideal weight for your dog should be. Young dogs are still growing, while old dogs are just getting heavier. Dogs that work for a living or who live in outdoor kennels all year require anywhere from 10 percent to 100 percent more calories than sedentary dogs living indoors. The female of a breed, as a rule, is somewhat smaller in bone structure and therefore should be fed a little less than her male counterpart. Dogs who are outdoors in cold weather will eat more than those who almost never get out.

On a general basis, here are a few guidelines for ideal weight by breed and size. Very small breeds such as Chihuahuas, Pekinese, and Miniature Schnauzers should weigh between 4 and 15 pounds. Of the small breeds, the Boston Terriers and Cocker Spaniels should weigh between 19 and 25 pounds. Of the medium breeds the Beagles, Brittany Spaniels and Siberian Huskies should weigh between 30 and 55 pounds. In the large breed category, the Airedales should weigh 50 pounds; Standard Poodle, 55; Pointers, 65; Golden Retrievers, 70; and Labrador Retrievers, 70 pounds. The very large breeds weigh considerably more. Old English Sheepdogs should weigh approximately 95 pounds; Great Pyrenees, 115; Great Danes, 130; Newfoundlands, 140; and St. Bernards, 165.

For most dogs, obesity starts in puppyhood, with little or no knowledge of nutrition on the part of the owner. The entire situation can be summed up in one word: overfeeding. If a puppy or young dog is fed table scraps, then the quantity of food he eats depends on the human appetite and how much has gone uneaten at the dinner table.

Look your dog over and watch for visible fat protrusions, such as a hanging stomach, double and triple chins, loose flesh around the collar, or a shapeless torso that is one solid cylinder shape from neck to tail. If any or all of these conditions exist, your dog is fat.

An important way to check your dog for obesity is to check what's happening around the animal's rib cage. Feel around the underside of your dog's trunk, which is his chest. Run your palm along the ribs on each side of the cage. A healthy, normal dog does not have too much tissue between the skin and the ribs. It is easy to feel each and every rib on a dog of normal weight. There should be just enough tissue to make a slight finger indentation when pressed against the rib, no more. To be precise, one fifth of an inch of tissue covering the ribs is the acceptable amount. Anything more than this indicates an overweight dog. This is especially true when the ribs cannot be felt or seen in outline form.

Obesity is almost always a feeding problem created when the older dog was just a puppy. Fat comes from eating more calories than one burns off during the course of a normal day's routine of physical and mental activity. Because the first year for a dog is one of intense growth, the novice dog owner witnesses the animal devouring every morsel available. This is misinterpreted as a permanent way of feeding. In addition, food is offered as a reward, as a symbol of love, affection, acceptance, and happiness. For these unfortunate animals, food becomes something beyond nutritional fuel for the body's needs. Eating turns into a habit, an obsession, an addiction. Studies of obese dogs have shown that 44 percent of the obese dogs observed were owned by obese humans.

There are several options for reducing your dog's weight. First, you can simply reduce your dog's diet by 40, 50, or even 60 percent. Many veterinarians will suggest this. Second, there are several commercially prepared food products designed to feed the dog with fewer calories. These are excellent products and do help satisfy your dog's appetite while reducing his caloric intake.

The nutritional requirements of dogs have been scientifically determined as a general set of principles. Each dog's body chemistry, however, is different and therefore uses nutritional intake in its own unique manner and style. However, enough is known to give every dog owner the knowledge to sufficiently feed every dog under most circumstances, allowing for the necessary adjustments for individual dogs. Here, then, is a scientific compromise for feeding dogs made necessary by domestication.

Feeding a dog commercially prepared food is fine, but figuring out the exact quantity to give can be elusive and complicated. Two beagles the same size, height, and weight may vary greatly in their use of food. One dog can eat 20 calories per pound of body weight and get fat, while the other may eat 37 calories per pound of food and remain slim. In other words, the caloric requirements differ from dog to dog, and that may simply relate to the peculiarities of a given dog's body chemistry—let alone his environment, state of health, or activity level.

Dog owners should make an estimated judgment as to what is the optimum body weight for his or her pet.

Use the following general feeding formula and weigh the dog once a week to determine if weight is gained, lost, or maintained; then adjust the food amount according to the dog's need to gain, lose, or maintain weight. Prescribed amounts of commercial dog food based on quantities are not accurate unless you know the caloric count of the food involved in terms of a measured quantity. Canned dog foods vary in caloric count from 400 calories per can to 650 and 700 calories per can. Dry food will also vary, but within a narrower range; from 1,500 calories to 2,000 calories per pound. When you convert calories to measured cups, you must do it on the basis of the caloric count of the individual product, and that information is not always on the label.

When deciding how much to feed your overweight dog, consider the following:

• One can of average dog food will feed approximately 20 pounds of dog per day (based on 500 or 550 calories per 20 pounds).

• One pound of dry food will feed approximately 60 to 65 pounds of dog per day. Five ounces of dry food will feed about 20 pounds of dog per day.

• One patty of soft-moist (burger type) food is approximately equal to ½ can of dog food. One packet will equal approximately 1 can of dog food. Thus, one patty will feed approximately 10 pounds of dog per day.

But dogs live different lifestyles and are often in varied states of health. In the winter, an outdoor dog's caloric requirements may increase by as much as 40 percent. When feeding puppies, allow them to eat as much as they want during the growth period (from weaning to six or eight months, and in larger breeds, even longer). This is called *ad libitum*, or self-feeding. Always replenish the puppy's food bowl when it is empty. (Dry food and supplements are the most practical type for this plan.) A pregnant bitch should be fed her normal maintenance diet until the end of the sixth week of gestation. During the last three weeks, food must be increased by approximately 25 or 30 percent. During the six weeks of lactation she may increase her food intake by almost three times her normal maintenance quantity. This quantity must be made available for the proper maintenance of good health.

Feeding a dog a proper diet, one that maintains the animal without producing excessive weight gain or loss, is probably the most important kindness a human can give to that pet. Good nutrition promises long life, good health, and a happy relationship. It is always best to consult your veterinarian for definitive information regarding your dog's individual needs.

Jumping on Furniture. This behavior is only a problem if you do not like competing with your dog for the recliner in your living room or a place on the couch. There are many dog owners who do not mind that their house pets spend the better part of the day on the furniture. However, there are many more dog owners who do not like to see this behavior, especially when it involves sudden leaps onto a chair while someone is sitting on it.

Allowing your dog on the furniture is inconsistent with the idea that dogs must be subordinate and humans must be dominant. You will never get your dog under control if the human/pet relationship does not embrace this concept.

Dogs like to jump on the furniture for several reasons. First, they like to jump. It is an opportunity to stretch the legs and move around a bit from an otherwise sedentary existence. The action consumes some of their excess energy, depending on the frequency and intensity of the jumping. Of course, they jump on the furniture in order to stretch out on it and be comfortable. It is nicer to sit on a soft sofa than the hard floor. It is also more interesting for them to be seated at a higher level than the floor. From their perspective, it gives them equal status with the human members of the family and that can create other behavior problems. It is difficult to control a dog that believes he has equal status with you.

When dogs jump on furniture it also has something to do with claiming territory, as well as advancing their position in the pecking order. If you allow a dog to jump on a piece of furniture and spend an hour or two on it every day, he is going to claim it as his own, as if it were his food bowl or his dog crate. When that happens it is difficult to wrench him off and reclaim the chair for yourself. It also makes him less willing to obey you. And then there is the unpleasantness of never knowing when your dog is going to jump on you or a guest at some inappropriate time. It is, altogether, very unacceptable behavior and should be discontinued.

Solutions to Jumping on Furniture

1) Have your dog obedience-trained. This gets him under control. An obedience-trained dog will respond properly to your commands, especially when you catch him in the act of jumping on your furniture. Obedience training establishes the proper relationship of human dominance and canine subordination. You will not have to shout hysterically or lose control of yourself in order to take charge of your dog's behavior.

2) Get a dog crate. Next to obedience training, using a dog crate during this problem-solving period is the most important step you can take. This is because you must first confine your puppy or grown dog when you are not there in order to prevent him from indulging himself on your furniture.

3) Learn how to administer a leash correction for when you catch your dog on the furniture or when he actually jumps on it. (See Chapter Five, "Getting Your Dog Under Control.")

The most basic problem-solving technique to stop this behavior is to set the stage for a jumping situation so that you can correct your dog for his misbehavior.

Take the dog to the living room or wherever the furniture is that he likes to jump on. Place a leash and training collar on him and leave the room (leave the house if necessary). When he jumps on his favorite chair and makes himself comfortable, swiftly enter the room, take hold of his leash and say "NO" several times, in a loud, firm tone of voice. As you do this, employ a leash correction, a firm snap and release of the leash, which tightens the training collar around the dog's neck for an instant and is then released. This must be followed by praise for the dog as you lead him off the furniture. The praise both reassures him that he is still in your good graces and rewards him for getting down. It reinforces the correction and is an essential part of the technique. (Follow the *correction* instructions for this technique properly, as outlined in Chapter Five, "Getting Your Dog Under Control.")

Lead the dog off the furniture and walk him (in the proper HEEL command) to his own sleeping or resting place or to his dog crate. Say, "Duke, HEEL. Good Dog." Give him the command SIT and then DOWN and then STAY, and walk away. Don't forget to praise your dog after giving each and every command. (Refer to the specifics of these commands in Chapter Five, "Getting Your Dog Under Control.")

4) Say, "NO" each and every time you see the dog jump on the furniture or whenever you find him sitting there. Make him get down. It seems obvious, but is eventually effective as a technique.

5) Some dogs will jump on the furniture when you are not home and then jump off as you come in the door. It is impossible to catch such clever dogs in the act of their misbehavior. Your best way to solve this variation of the problem is to create a dislike for the furniture.

You can do this by sitting on the sofa and bursting a balloon next to the dog and saying, "NO" in a loud, firm tone of voice. This should startle him and make him shy away from the balloon. Next, tape many blown-up balloons onto the furniture and leave. If the dog was sufficiently startled by the popped balloon, he will shy away from the furniture. Do this for a week or two in order to create the habit of not jumping where he doesn't belong.

A variation of this method is to use four or five spring-snap mouse traps on the furniture. Of course, you don't want to hurt the dog, so you must cover the set traps with three thicknesses of newspaper and tape them down. If the dog hops onto the furniture the traps will go off and snap loudly. The sound should startle the dog and make the experience unpleasant.

Another variation for making him dislike the furniture is to spread sheets of aluminum foil over it and tape it down. The crinkling sound and slippery texture may turn him off.

You might also try tying a rope across each piece of furniture with several soda cans attached to it. Fill each can with marbles or coins so that they make noise when they are shaken. If the dog jumps he will shake the rope and rattle the cans. The noise may just be too unpleasant for him. You may be able to create your own method of getting your dog to dislike the furniture. There are commercial products available that spray a scent on the furniture that is unpleasant to the dog but imperceptible to humans. It is worth a try.

Jumping on People. The way we relate to our puppies teaches them how to behave positively or negatively later on when they grow up. Adorable puppy behavior is often unacceptable once the dog becomes full grown. Your new dog adores you and everything else connected with you—including your face, which he is always trying to reach for a slurping kiss on the lips. Now, that may be perfectly fine for you, but what if you are wearing a black, silk evening dress with pearl accessories. You wouldn't want muddy paw marks, scratches and wrinkles on it just before going out. And what about your friends and neighbors who get jumped up on when they don't even like dogs? Jumping on people is just not proper behavior for a grown dog and it begins in puppyhood.

Like most behavioral problems, this one is preventable. Ideally, even a puppy should be required to behave himself, taking into consideration, of course, his young age. This comes through instruction, leadership and determined insistence. But most important of all is not encouraging behavior that becomes negative later on. Obviously, an obedience-trained dog behaves much better than one who is not. But such problem behavior as jumping on people is too often the result of humans' unwittingly encouraging, and even teaching, such behavior. When you carry a puppy around all the time, kneel down for him to jump in your lap, sit on the furniture with him, pet him, or give him treats for jumping on your legs, you are teaching him that it is fine to jump on you later on. If you do not want your grown dog to jump on you or anyone else, then do not allow him to do it as a puppy. Bear in mind that wolves and wild dogs that jump on one another do it with either sexual or aggressive implications.

Solutions to Jumping on People

1) You must decide early in the game whether your dog is allowed to jump on you and others. If not, never allow your puppy to jump on you or anyone else for any reason whatsoever. Do not allow your puppy to jump on your leg. Do not carry your puppy (or grown dog) around in your arms as you would a baby. It must be understood that a dog cannot distinguish between who he is allowed to jump on and who he is not allowed to jump on. If you allow him to jump on you in order to kiss you, then he is going to jump on everyone he wants to greet, and that can get both of you in trouble.

2) When a dog jumps on you he is at your eye level and, in his mind, equal to you. This contradicts the entire concept of dominance-subordination. Have your dog obedience-trained. This gets him under control. An obedience-trained dog will respond properly to your commands, especially when he jumps on people. Obedience training establishes the proper relationship of human dominance and canine subordination. If your dog is properly trained you will not have to shout hysterically or lose control of yourself in order to take charge of his behavior.

3) Learn how to administer a leash correction for when your dog jumps on someone. (See Chapter Five, "Getting Your Dog Under Control.")

The most basic problem-solving technique to stop this behavior is to set the stage for a jumping situation so that you can correct your dog's misbehavior.

Take the dog outdoors or wherever he is most likely to jump on someone. Place a leash and training collar on him and take him for a walk. Have a friend walk toward you and greet you enthusiastically. If the dog jumps on your friend, firmly jerk the leash to the side (as outlined in Chapter Five) and say "NO" several times, in a loud, firm tone of voice. The leash correction administers a firm snap and release of the leash, which tightens the training collar around the dog's neck for an instant and is then released. This must be followed by praise for the dog. The praise both reassures him that he is still in your good graces and rewards him for getting down. It reinforces the correction and is an essential part of the technique. (Follow the correction instructions for this technique properly as outlined in Chapter Five.)

You may then either give the dog the commands "SIT" and "STAY," or lead him away with the proper HEEL command. Say, "Duke, HEEL. Good Dog." Continue walking down the street and then try the exercise several times a day. Do not forget to praise your dog after giving each and every command. (Refer to the specifics of these commands in Chapter Five.)

4) Say, "NO" each and every time the dog jumps on you or anyone else. Praise him immediately afterwards. The verbal correction will eventually work without the leash correction.

With this correction method it is not necessary to use abusive techniques used by others in the dark ages, such as stepping on the dog's hind toes when he jumps or kneeing him in the chest. These are brutal acts that can injure your dog and ruin your relationship with him. It is not pleasant to have a dog that fears you.

Mounting. Young, male dogs (including some puppies) may engage in a form of masturbation described as mounting. Unlike females, such dogs may become aroused at any time by too much handling in play or expressions of affection, over socialization, various scents, or other unknown stimuli. Their erotic desires are usually expressed by a simulation of sexual intercourse using the human leg as a substitute for the female dog, with a humping motion. This behavior is distressing to most pet owners and can also become somewhat dangerous. It is difficult to stop such behavior once it begins and often becomes aggressive. A male dog in the act of sexual intercourse is a dominant animal and ignores the demand of human dominance and canine subordination. Because mounting can lead to injury and a disintegration of the proper human/pet relationship, it is a form of misbehavior that must be corrected promptly.

Solving the Mounting Problem

1) Have your dog obedience-trained. This gets him under control. An obedience trained dog will respond properly to your commands, especially when he attempts to mount someone's leg. Obedience training establishes the proper relationship of human dominance and canine subordination. If your dog is properly trained you will not have to shout hysterically or lose control of yourself in order to correct his behavior.

2) Learn how to administer a leash correction for when your dog attempts to mount someone's leg. (See Chapter Five, "Getting Your Dog Under Control.")

The most basic problem-solving technique to stop this behavior is to patiently wait for the misbehavior to occur, so that you can correct your dog firmly and decisively.

Take the dog to wherever he is most likely to exhibit this behavior. Place a leash and training collar on him. Have the person to whom he is attracted (it could be you or just about anyone) sit on the sofa in order to set up the situation. If the dog displays his misbehavior, firmly jerk the leash to the side (as outlined in Chapter Five) and say "NO" several times, in a loud, firm tone of voice. The leash correction involves a firm snap and release of the leash, which tightens the training collar around the dog's neck for an instant and is then released. This must be followed by praise for the dog. The praise both reassures him that he is still in your good graces and rewards him for getting down. It reinforces the correction and is an essential part of the technique. (Follow the correction instructions for this technique properly as outlined in Chapter Five.)

You may then either give the dog the commands, "SIT" and "STAY," or lead him away with the proper HEEL command. Say, "Duke, HEEL. Good Dog." Continue walking around the house or out on the street and then try the exercise several times a day. Do not forget to praise your dog after giving each and every command. Refer to the specifics of these commands in Chapter Five.

3) Avoid such play behavior as jumping on you, inviting the dog onto your lap, or holding him upright by his front paws. Some dogs are stimulated by close contact with women experiencing their menstrual cycle. During such times it is best to keep your distance.

Males dogs are always stimulated by the scent of a female dog in heat. Avoid this situation if possible. Male dogs can also become masturbatory on occasion once they have become sexually experienced with other dogs.

For the male that is constantly mounting human legs, vertical objects, or children, the best and most humane solution is castration. A castrated male dog is a wonderful pet that becomes sharply focused on his human family without any sexual misbehavior.

Sexual Misbehavior. It is a natural part of a dog's life to mate and to reproduce puppies, but every species in nature has been programmed to conform to its own sexual activity. Almost all male dogs will attempt to mate with a female in heat. It has been the experience of many dog owners that their male house dogs have had certain changes of personality after one or two matings. They can become more dominant, more territorial, less playful, less tolerant. This is not always the case, but it remains a distinct possibility and should be considered before allowing a house pet to mate.

The sexuality of the female is much different. Unless she is spayed, whether she likes it or not, she will come into season twice a year and experience a hormonal and chemical change in her body at that time. A female usually experiences her estrous cycle every six months, and it normally lasts a total of twenty-one days. During the first week there is a bloody discharge which becomes somewhat colorless in the second week and disappears during the third and final week. This happens whether the dog is ever mated or not. During the three weeks of estrus, twice a year, it is necessary to seclude the animal so that no males can get at her. The best method is to board her at a kennel. If she is to remain at home, she should be kept under lock and key so that there is not the remotest chance of her darting away and mating with a neighborhood dog. If the dog is not going to be shown in the ring or bred for puppies, having her spayed between six months and four years of age solves most problems pertaining to sex.

Anyone who has ever loved an animal will be appalled to know that approximately ten thousand puppies and kittens are born every hour, with the result that twenty million dogs and cats are abandoned and impounded every year. Of these unwanted, helpless creatures, 90 percent are euthanized. Destroying life in such great quantities costs society more than large sums of money: the effect can be morally and psychologically toxic. The fact is that there are more dogs in the world than there are homes for them, even though close to 50 million dogs make their homes with human families.

In light of this, birth control becomes a vitally important issue. This term is not usually applied to pets, but any loving dog owner will recognize it as the only way to curtail a burgeoning population of the unwanted and all its attendant woes. Sophisticated pet owners also know that the joys of cuddling and playing with puppies soon fade when the reality of a pet's sexual maturity becomes apparent some time late in the first year of its life. To the human experiencing pet ownership for the first time, this unaccustomed behavior almost always comes as a disturbing surprise. Equally disturbing is the realization that such behavior will be recurring regularly for the rest of the animal's life, unless something is done about it. So this is one more reason to investigate the various forms of birth control that eliminate these domestically disruptive sessions.

Probably the most important and effective form of pet birth control is surgical sterilization. In the female this is known as *spaying* or *ovariohysterectomy* and involves the removal of the animal's ovaries. For male dogs the procedure is known as *castration*. Animals that have been surgically sterilized are referred to as *altered*, *neutered*, or *fixed*. Contrary to popular belief, altered dogs do not become fat, nor do they lose their personalities, although altered males lose some of their aggressiveness and other nasty traits.

Surgical neutering of dogs is the most popular form of birth control and is 100 percent effective. The major drawback (if it is a drawback) is that it is irreversible. The fact that most veterinarians agree that spayed females are less prone to perianal adenoma (tumor) is another positive argument to support these procedures. Methods of birth control other than surgical neutering are being pursued by various researchers for both male and female pets. Implants, chemically treated pet food, chemical castration, and hormonal manipulation are all being studied in research laboratories around the world. The prospects for a variety of birth control techniques are good. But until such time as a totally effective technique is developed, surgical sterilization, a closed door, or a strong leash are still the best birth control devices around.

Stealing Food. This is a bit of behavior that seems harmless from a puppy or young dog but is quite annoying and costly from a full-grown one. Some dogs have the audacity to place their front paws up on a person in order to get at what they are eating. If you pull away you could even make the dog aggressive and snappy. Someone could get hurt, and it could be you.

Make no mistake, all but the obedience-trained dogs will go for something that smells good. There are two aspects to handling this situation. First, it must be a fixed rule that the dog is never hand fed. This should especially apply to the kitchen and dining areas, where the dog is likely to beg for food. Begging for food is out completely. The dog must always be fed from his bowl. Second, the dog must be consistently and firmly corrected each and every time there is an incident involving food.

How, you may ask, can this be accomplished unless the leash is attached to the collar at all times? If the dog collar is on (and it should be at all times), you can make an improvised correction by tugging the collar to the side in a firm manner and saying, "NO," several times in a no-nonsense tone of voice. Once the dog is down, be nice and say, "Good girl." Correction without praise immediately afterward is ineffective.

Solutions to Stealing Food

1) Have your dog obedience-trained. This gets him under control. An obedience trained dog will respond properly to your commands, especially when he misbehaves, such as stealing food from a kitchen counter. Obedience training establishes the proper relationship of human dominance and canine subordination. If your dog is properly trained you will not have to shout hysterically or lose control of yourself in order to correct his behavior. (Refer to Chapter Five, "Getting Your Dog Under Control.")

2) A more precise way of ending this problem is setting up the situation under controlled conditions and then giving a proper correction. Place the leash and training collar on the dog (see Chapter Five). Allow the dog to walk around with them on for fifteen or twenty minutes. Then take your dog into the kitchen where you have placed a piece of raw meat on the counter, or in some area that is accessible to him. Leave the room and watch the situation from an obscured location. The instant the dog goes for the food, rush in, grab the leash, and tug it hard to the right, then release it instantly. As you tug the leash say, "NO" several times in a firm tone of voice. Once the dog has recovered from the surprise, give him immediate praise. Then walk the dog to his own food bowl, hold it up to him, and once again offer praise. This is a teaching technique as well as a corrective technique. A food stealing problem must not be allowed to develop into a steady habit. The problem must be dealt with swiftly and firmly.

8

THE AMERICAN KENNEL CLUB'S "CANINE GOOD CITIZEN TEST"

The American Kennel Club (at the suggestion of, and with input from, dog writer Herm David) has created and developed the Canine Good Citizen Program (CGC) in response to anticanine sentiment which has been gaining momentum. The program was launched in September, 1989 and has steadily gained enormous acceptance from a broad spectrum of dog organizations, such as the ASPCA, Responsible Dog Owners of America, and The Delta Society, to name but a few. Given the thousands upon thousands of pure-bred and mixed breed dogs that have successfully completed the CGC program, it is clear that dog owners everywhere have embraced it with open arms.

According to James E. Dearinger, Vice-President, Obedience Department, Kennel Club and author of the testing program material that follows, dogs are being tested at the rate of approximately one thousand a month. Secretary Dearinger writes in the Canine Good Citizen Program pamphlet:

"The American Kennel Club's Canine Good Citizen Test focuses entirely on good dog manners but, more especially, responsible pet ownership, and conveys through acceptable behavior what is expected of all dogs in the community."

The Making of a Canine Good Citizen

When man took the dog from the wild as his companion, he assumed responsibility for the dog's care and upbringing. Over time, man taught dogs to perform certain tasks and to comply with household rules so that life together would be mutually satisfying. Today, dogs in this country must have good manners to live harmoniously within families and to survive the increasing challenges of anticanine advocates.

Every dog should know at least four basic commands in order to function acceptably in public: HEEL, SIT, DOWN, and STAY. An understanding of these commands creates social skills which defuse anticanine feelings and reflect positively on all dogs. Knowledge of these commands fosters good citizenship. However, your dog is not capable of training itself; it needs your help to become a "Canine Good Citizen."

Training results in a controlled dog, one which does not bother the neighbors or their dogs, and does not balk at grooming procedures or a veterinarian's examination. Training stimulates your dog's intelligence, and lends stability and meaning to its life by letting it know how to please you and what you expect. In an emergency, training can save its life.

A dog that possesses a social demeanor reflects favorably on its owner, its breed, and its species. The American Kennel Club's Canine Good Citizen Program exists to help you and dog owners everywhere achieve this goal and be recognized for your accomplishment.

An increasing number of AKC clubs and obedience schools throughout the country offer courses that prepare you and your dog for the Canine Good Citizen Test. These courses allow you and your dog to work with others who share the same goal. Many of these groups sponsor a test upon completion of the course.

If a course is not available in your area, you and your dog can work together with the material from this chapter. When you have finished, we hope you will seek certification for your dog, who will then join the ranks of thousands that have attained the "Canine Good Citizen" certification.

Purpose

The purpose of the Canine Good Citizen Test is to demonstrate that the dog, as a companion, can be a respected member of the community, and can be trained and conditioned always to behave in the home, in public places, and in the presence of other dogs in a manner that reflects favorably on the owner and the dog.

The Canine Good Citizen Test is not a competitive obedience program and does not require precision in the execution of exercises. It is a certification program involving everyday situations in a relaxed atmosphere. It seeks to identify and officially recognize those dogs that possess the attributes that enable them to serve effectively as personal companions and members in good standing within the community.

Sponsor

Any AKC Club of record or any qualified dog training organizations, as well as 4-H Clubs, private trainers, and others may hold a Canine Good Citizen Test.

Evaluators

Any person can be an evaluator, but evaluators should be experienced in working with and training dogs in obedience, or for shows, or for the field.

In the interest of time and maintaining spectator appeal, three evaluators should be employed as follows:

First evaluator conducts test number one;

Second evaluator conducts tests two through nine;

Third evaluator conducts test number ten.

Evaluating the Dog

The evaluator must have considerable knowledge of dog behavior. He or she must have experience in working with and training dogs, and a keen awareness of the public's attitude toward dogs.

Before the evaluator passes the dog, he or she should consider if the dog is:

1) The kind of dog you would like to own;
2) The kind of dog that would be safe with children;
3) The kind of dog you would welcome as a neighbor;
4) The kind of dog that makes its owner happy and is not making someone else unhappy.

Qualifying

Dogs are evaluated on the basis of "pass-fail." In order to qualify for the Canine Good Citizen award, a dog must pass each of the ten test categories. The dog need only pass this test once in order to receive a Canine Good Citizen

Certificate. Any dog that eliminates during testing must be marked "failed."

Dismissal

Any dog which growls, snaps, bites, attacks, or attempts to attack any person, or another dog, shall be dismissed from the test.

Collars, Leads, and Equipment

All dogs should wear well-fitting buckle or slip collars of either leather, fabric, or chain, in addition to items specified in Test #1. Special training collars such as pinch collars are not acceptable. The lead should be either leather or fabric.

Note: All tests are performed on leash.

Tests

1) Appearance and Grooming

The evaluator will inspect the dog to determine if it is clean and groomed. The dog must appear to be in healthy condition (i.e., of proper weight, clean, healthy, and alert). The owner must present a current rabies certificate and any other state or locally required inoculation certificate or license. This part of the test demonstrates the owner's care, concern, and responsibility. The evaluator then combs or brushes the dog lightly and in a natural manner to show the dog's willingness to be groomed and to permit someone other than his handler to do so. The handler should supply the comb or brush commonly used on the dog. The evaluator then lightly examines the ears and gently picks up each front foot. It is not necessary for the dog to hold a specific position while the examination is in progress, and the handler may talk to the dog, praise, and give encouragement throughout the exercise.

This is a practical test, demonstrating that the dog will welcome being groomed and examined, and will permit a stranger, such as a veterinarian or groomer, to do so.

Training for Test #1

Gradual, positive introduction to grooming and examining procedures should begin as soon as your dog enters your home. Gentle combing and brushing are a natural extension to petting and stroking. If your dog fears this type of handling, or becomes uncertain when its ears or feet are touched, you should spend time allowing it to associate grooming and human touch with a positive experience, such as vocal praise or training treats, for the slightest proper response.

Positive daily handling and grooming help you recognize physical problems early, and your dog will learn that being examined and groomed are part of every day life. Once your dog is comfortable being groomed and examined by you, you can ask others to do the same, using commands of "SIT," "DOWN," or "STAND," if you wish. Your dog is now ready for upcoming visits to pet care professionals and for Canine Good Citizen Test #1.

2) Accepting a Stranger

The principal feature of this test is to demonstrate that a dog will allow a stranger to approach the handler and dog in a natural everyday situation.

The evaluator walks up to the dog and handler and greets the handler in a friendly manner, ignoring the dog.

The evaluator and handler shake hands and exchange pleasantries. The dog must show no sign of resentment or shyness, and must not break position or try to go to the evaluator.

Training for Test #2

Your dog needs to be shown how to behave when you meet friends on the street or welcome them into your home. No one enjoys a lunging, jumping dog, and many individuals are afraid of such an animal.

You need to arrange numerous social encounters by inviting friends to your home or by taking walks in your neighborhood. Keep your leash handy when you are working in your home so that you can snap it on your dog as soon as the doorbell rings. When your dog shows signs of excitement at the approach of an individual, snap back quickly on the collar to stop any lunging, pulling, or attempts to jump, and accompany this with a sharp vocal reprimand. Praise your dog when he responds.

Have your dog "SIT" at heel and "STAY" if you wish as you pause to shake hands (see training for Tests 6 and 7). "STAY" helps to keep excitable dogs under control. Praise when it obeys, and correct instantly if it attempts to break position. It may take many repetitions to impress on your dog that social encounters at home or in public must be met in a civilized way. If you are consistent in imparting the behavior you expect as you meet friends and strangers, your dog soon will respond with dignified aplomb.

3) Walk on Loose Lead—Out for a Walk

The principal feature of this test is to demonstrate that the handler is in control. The dog must be on the left side of the handler (the left side position is required in all activities where the dog serves man, such as guide dogs for the blind, Canine Corps, etc.). The dog need not be in the "HEEL" position as required by AKC Obedience tests. Ideally, the position should be such as to leave no doubt that the dog's attention is on the handler and that it responds to movements and changes of direction by the handler.

The evaluator may use a preplotted course, or may direct the team by issuing instructions or commands. In either case, there must be a left turn, right turn, and about turn, with at least one halt in between and another at the end. The handler may talk to the dog throughout, praise, and help or command the dog to SIT if desired at the halts.

Training for Test #3

In order to see your movements and respond to them, your dog's head needs to be fairly close to your left side. The vast majority of untrained dogs tend to forge ahead, making a simple walk an unpleasant task. Your dog can learn to move on a loose lead, and as soon as it does you will find that you are taking it everywhere with you because it is fun to be with.

You can train for this exercise in a traditional way by allowing your dog slack in the leash as you begin to move, then snapping back sharply or making a sharp turn with an accompanying snap and release as soon as the dog begins to pull ahead. Always release the tension immediately after snapping the lead. When your dog is brought back near your leg and is moving without pulling, be sure to praise it. With this technique, it learns that you snap when it starts to pull. Your praise and the feeling of a loose collar when it is near your leg will be very reinforcing. As you progress, you can make sharper turns to keep its attention on you. When you stop, so should the dog. It is not necessary that it SIT when you halt, but a SIT gives you much more control in public, especially if you are approaching people who will want to talk to you.

You can also teach this exercise in an inductive fashion by showing your dog a treat or a toy when you want it to move, as you begin to walk. Inductive training has the advantage of requiring fewer corrections because the dog is motivated to stay in the proper place in anticipation of food or play, as well as the reinforcements of praise and a loose collar. Eventually, the dog develops a habit of moving happily in the desired position and treats and toys can be eliminated.

Whatever technique you use should result in success, especially if you bring in distractions gradually. However, quite often handlers working on their own really need the help and advice of an experienced trainer to teach this exercise effectively. This exercise requires fast reflexes and just the right touch on the leash and collar. If you run into a problem, try a trainer.

4) Walk Through a Crowd

The principal feature of this test is to demonstrate that the dog has no difficulty in moving about in pedestrian traffic.

The dog and handler walk around and pass close to several people (at least three), demonstrating that the dog is conditioned to behave at all times and is under control in public places. The dog may show some interest in the strangers, but should continue to walk with the handler without evidence of shyness or resentment. The dog should not be straining at the leash. The handler may talk to the dog, and encourage or praise the dog throughout the exercise.

Training for Test #4

If you have been practicing loose leash walking in your neighborhood, you are probably going to accomplish this exercise as part of your daily workout because you are apt to encounter people. If there is no one around, go into town or to the local playground. If you have an excitable dog, try to work up to close encounters gradually until your dog is comfortable. For example, choose a quiet weekday evening for a walk in town before you choose a busy weekend. You can also practice your loose leash walking at a distance from people and then move in closer as your dog adjusts to their presence. Correct your dog with a collar snap if it attempts to pull, reaches out to sniff at, or jumps on passing individuals. Praise the dog when it is good. With experience, it will learn to ignore pedestrians.

5) Sit for Exam

The principal feature of this test is to demonstrate that the dog will allow the approach of a stranger and permit petting.

With the dog sitting at the handler's left side throughout the exercise, the evaluator approaches and proceeds to pet the dog on the head and body only. The handler may talk to his dog throughout the exercise.

The dog must not show shyness or resentment. The evaluator then circles the dog and handler, completing the test.

Training for Test #5

In public, strangers are going to want to meet your budding "Canine Good Citizen." You have already accomplished a large part of this exercise by teaching it to ignore pedestrians, and to react calmly to individuals visiting at home and in public.

Start this exercise by having your dog remain sitting while you and family members approach and pet it. Then practice with people the dog knows and likes. Correct your dog instantly if it starts to jump up or otherwise break position. Praise it when it is good.

As soon as your dog understands that it must hold the sit while being petted by those it knows, you can allow strangers to do the same. Remember that many individuals, especially children, do not know how to approach animals and may need some direction.

6) SIT and DOWN On Command

The principal feature of this test is to demonstrate that the dog has had some formal training and will respond to the handler's commands.

The handler may take a reasonable time and use more than one command to make the dog "SIT" and then "DOWN." The evaluator must determine if the dog has responded to the handler's commands. The handler may not force the dog into either position, but may touch the dog to offer gentle guidance.

Training for Test #6

If you are like most dog owners, you have already taught your dog to "SIT" on command. Maybe you have also taught your dog to "DOWN." If so, you can skip this section and go right to Test #7.

If your dog does not know these commands, you have probably discovered that you need the control that these two commands can provide.

These exercises can be taught in either a traditional or inductive fashion, and you will be successful with either one as long as you are consistent.

To teach your dog to SIT using a traditional approach,

place it at your left side, grasp the leash close to the collar with your right hand, and use your left hand to push quickly on its rear as you say the command. Praise when it responds. As soon as it learns to SIT, you can start the DOWN. With your dog seated, say the command and push lightly on the shoulders with your left hand while your right hand either pulls downward on the collar or moves under the chest behind the front legs to slide the legs forward. Praise as soon as it responds.

To teach your dog to SIT using an inductive method, hold a piece of food or a toy in front of its nose and slide it upwards over the nose and forehead, keeping it very close to its body, as you say the command. As it looks up at the reward, the rear will settle into a SIT. If it does not, take your free hand and push lightly on the rear. Praise and give the reward instantly. To teach the "DOWN," bring the food or toy in front of the nose and then lower it to the ground slightly ahead of its feet as you say the command. As it reaches down for the reward, it will lower the front end of the body into a prone position to receive the reward. If it does not lower completely into a DOWN position, use your free hand to push lightly on the shoulders. Praise and reward instantly.

Practice these two exercises several times in a row over a period of several days, then gradually bring in distractions until your dog responds reliably to either command in public situations.

7) Stay in Position (SIT or DOWN)

The principal feature of this test is to demonstrate that the dog will assume and remain in the position commanded by the handler (SIT or DOWN position being the option of the handler).

The handler may use more than one command to get the dog into position, using a reasonable length of time to do so. The handler then gives a command for the dog to "STAY" and, when instructed by the evaluator, drops the leash and walks forward about twenty feet, turns, and returns to the dog at a natural pace.

The dog must maintain the position in which it was left until the handler returns and until the evaluator instructs the handler to release the dog from its position.

Training for Test #7

With your dog at your left side, command it to "SIT" or "DOWN." Once it is in position, you are ready to enforce a "STAY" command. Lower your left hand, palm towards the dog's face, as a signal to stay as you give the "STAY" command. Pivot right in front of its nose. Remain there for a few seconds, repositioning your dog instantly if it starts to break position with an accompanying, "NO! SIT (DOWN)! STAY!" as you do so. Then pivot back to its side and praise the dog. If you have discovered that an inductive method works best for you, give your dog a treat or a toy to play with as you praise. Repeat the exercise several times over a period of several days.

As soon as your dog understands the concept of this exercise, start adding time (about ten seconds per day) and then bring in distractions. Only when it is reliable under distracted conditions for a period of 1-3 minutes on a sit and 3-5 minutes on a down should you begin to increase the distance. Move in closer and reduce time if you experience difficulty, and be sure to use the commands whenever and wherever you want them enforced. Before you know it, you will wonder how you and your dog ever managed to live together without the SIT, DOWN, or STAY command.

8) Reaction to Another Dog

The principal feature of this test is to demonstrate the proper behavior when in the presence of other dogs. Two handlers and their dogs approach each other from a distance of about ten yards, stop, shake hands and exchange pleasantries, and continue on about five yards.

The dogs should demonstrate no more than casual interest. Neither dog should go to the other dog or handler.

Training for Test #8

If you are working alone, and there are few people in your neighborhood who walk their dogs, you will need to locate areas where dogs will be, such as a boarding kennel, grooming salon, or veterinarian's office. These places offer opportunities to impart good canine-to-canine manners, and are also locations in which you need control.

If you have already accomplished the STAY exercise with distractions, you can consider this exercise as just one more example of a distraction. To begin, every time you see a dog and handler walking, enforce a "STAY" command in either a SIT or DOWN position as they pass by. Correct your dog instantly if it breaks position, and praise it when it responds. Start from a safe distance, moving as far away as need be so that both dogs in the encounter feel secure. When your dog becomes confident, you can move closer to approaching dogs and handlers. If anyone wants to stop and talk, enforce your "STAY" command.

Remember that in a Canine Good Citizen Test both dogs being tested have had an introduction to this exercise; in real life, the dog you are approaching may not be so fortunate. Do not be surprised if dog owners comment on your dog's good manners. Once again, you and your dog will be helping to educate the public. You may even find other dogs and handlers to train with!

Practice this exercise until your dog reacts reliably to canine encounters by ignoring the approaching dog and handler, allowing you to stop and shake hands, and go your own way.

9) Reactions to Distractions

The principal feature of this test is to determine that the dog is confident at all times when faced with distracting conditions.

The evaluator will select two of the following:

a) A person on crutches, or in a wheel chair, or using a walker. This test simulates a disabled person requiring such an aid;

b) Sudden closing or opening of a door;

c) Dropping a large book, no closer than ten feet behind the dog;

d) A jogger running in front of the dog;

e) Good-natured pushing and shoving or animated, excited talk and back-slapping by persons, with the dog and handler passing within ten feet;

f) A person pushing a shopping cart approaching from the front or rear, passing about six feet to the side of the dog;

g) A person on a bicycle approaching from the front or rear, passing about six feet to the side of the dog.

The dog may express natural interest and curiosity, and may startle, but should not panic, try to run away, show aggressiveness, or bark. The handler may talk to the dog, encourage, or praise it throughout the exercise.

Training for Test #9

Life is full of surprises and your dog should react calmly to most of them. Through exposure to everyday situations on an everyday basis, your dog will probably learn to ignore the type of distractions used in this test. If it rarely sees a bicycle, or has taken to barking and fence-running when it sees a jogger, you may be in for a surprise when you are with your dog in public and are presented with distractions such as these.

If your dog shows fear of unusual objects, sounds, or movements you should help by briefly exposing it to these things in a nonthreatening environment, preferably at a distance that is comfortable for it. Praise, treats, toys, and playful interaction may help take its mind off fear and help it associate what was once frightening with positive experiences. You can then gradually increase the duration and proximity as your dog becomes confident. For example, a heavy book dropped right behind a dog's back may cause an inexperienced or sound-sensitive dog to panic, but a heavy book dropped sixty feet in front of the same dog may not even be noticed. Gradually moving the book closer and behind the back will desensitize the dog in a positive way.

If your dog shows aggressive behavior, the same technique may be applied by exposing the dog gradually, and at a distance, to the things that trigger aggression. Correct instantly with a collar snap and verbal correction for unwanted behavior, and praise instantly for proper behavior. A dog of sound temperament learns quickly that unwarranted displays of antisocial behavior will not be tolerated.

10) Dog Left Alone

The principal feature of this test is that the dog may be left alone demonstrating training and good manners.

The handler will fasten the dog to a fifteen-foot line and go to a place out of sight of the dog for five minutes. The dog should not continually bark, whine, howl, pace unnecessarily, or register anything other than mild agitation or nervousness.

It should be noted that this test is designed to determine if the dog can be left alone without causing a stressful situation, and that AKC does not endorse tying out as a general practice. It should also be noted that this is not a STAY exercise, and dogs may stand, sit, lie down, and change position during this exercise.

Dogs should be tested individually and not as a group.

Training for Test #10

As you and your dog work together, you will discover a bond developing that is based on trust. Not only will you begin to trust your dog, but it will trust you and your judgment, even if it means the dog will be left alone in a strange place from time to time.

Prepare your dog by going out of sight for a few seconds as you practice distance on your "STAY" commands. You can walk behind a tree or around the corner of a building. If you elect to use a fifteen-foot lead and hold on to it, you will know if it moves even if you cannot see it. Correct your dog calmly if it breaks position or vocalizes, and repeat the exercise. If you "disappear" for only a few seconds, and never go any great distance, your dog will learn that you are never far away, even if it cannot see you.

As soon as your dog is comfortable with your going out of sight, you can stop enforcing a "STAY" command. Tie it at a convenient and safe location, and leave for a few seconds. The "STAY" command helps your dog concentrate and obey even if it feels uncertain. You might want to introduce a new command such as "WAIT HERE" or "I'LL

BE BACK" to help it understand what is expected—that it must not try to run away or vocalize, but need not remain in a specific posture.

Gradually increase the time that you are out of sight and add social distractions until you have worked up to five minutes.

Each participating dog and dog owner will be awarded a CGC certificate by the organization conducting the test "in recognition of successful completion of the American Kennel Club CANINE GOOD CITIZEN TEST." The certificate is suitable for framing and offers those who achieve it a prize worth displaying.

The CGC Test is just one of many programs offered by The American Kennel Club. The AKC's Public Education Department communicates with three thousand Public Educational Coordinators appointed by AKC Clubs across the country. This office has developed and made available videos, bumper stickers, and a number of brochures such as "Do You Really Want to Own a Dog," and "Should I Breed My Dog," to promote responsible dog ownership, as well as programs for youngsters, such as "Adopt-A-Vet Summer," and "Kids Canine Corner."

The American Kennel Club urges all dog owners to avail themselves of these programs, thereby assuring that the dog who shares our world will always be a welcome and respected member of the community.

For more information write to:

American Kennel Club
Attention: Performance Division
51 Madison Avenue
New York, New York 10010.